D0979275

WS
WOUNDED
SPIRITS

WOUNDED SPIRITS

A Biblical Approach to Dealing With the Effects of Post Traumatic Stress Disorder

DOUGLAS J. CARRAGHER, Th.D.
Sergeant Major, U.S. Army Retired

WaldenWay
PUBLICATIONS
PO Box 1099, Murfreesboro, TN 37133-1099

Copyright 2014 by
Revised 2017
WaldenWay Publications
A division of Sword of the Lord Publishers
ISBN 978-0-87398-985-5

All rights reserved. No part of this publication may be used or reproduced, stored in or introduced into a retrieval system, or transmitted in any form or by any means (printed, written, photocopied, electronic, audio or otherwise) without prior written permission of the publisher.

All Scripture quotations are from
the King James Bible.

Printed and Bound in the United States of America

Contents

Introduction

Wounded Spirits

> *"The spirit of a man will sustain his infirmity; but a wounded spirit who can bear?"*—Proverbs 18:14.

For many years the Lord has burdened my heart for people with wounded spirits. This study is for those affected by Post Traumatic Stress Disorder (PTSD). While this disorder has been getting attention only recently, it is not a new disease. Its causes, severe trauma and stress, date back to the beginning of man.

If you or someone you love is experiencing any of the following symptoms after a traumatic or stressful event, PTSD may be the problem: suicidal thoughts, anxiety, phobias, depression, insomnia, feelings of guilt, anger, irritability, bad dreams, flashbacks, and apathy.

Through these pages you will find how the Lord provides answers in His Word for these kinds of symptoms.

In this study, we will also examine real-life situations

and case studies as we seek to find answers using the Word of God.

This book is basically just a foundation, and most people will benefit from using this material in small-group sessions at a local church or in a home. After you have completed this book, we hope to assign you to a suitable group close to you. Contact me through afbmissions.com for information about a suitable group.

We are in the process of developing teams to train church leaders and those affected by PTSD. We want to help by introducing biblical concepts and more importantly by developing the framework for PTSD groups in churches, which can thereby in a dark world be lights for millions of sufferers.

Hopefully you, like many others, will find answers to the problems that have arisen in your life as a consequence of a severe personal traumatic event or events. I've found through the Lord's Word that He is all you need!

The Lord will use His Word to help you find answers. May the Lord bless you as you journey through this study.

Doug Carragher, Th.D.
Sergeant Major, U.S. Army Retired

Dr. Carragher's PTSD Testimony

The Lord used three key events in Dr. Carragher's life to demonstrate the need for this book.

As a young, noncommissioned officer, he witnessed a soldier drive a piece of heavy equipment over the side of a bridge into a small river, flipping it over so that the soldier was trapped underwater. Carragher tried to administer mouth-to-mouth resuscitation underwater, coming up to breathe in between breaths of life. The young man died.

Five years later while serving as a leader in the Quick Reaction Force at Fort Harrison, Indiana, he and his soldiers responded to a plane crash. An Air Force jet had crashed into a hotel lobby, killing nine people and injuring others. Though the team was sent to guard sensitive equipment, they were needed to recover the bodies of the nine victims. Each face was a horrifying image.

The last event the Lord used to shape this book occurred on October 15, 1993. After participating in extreme Army physical training, Carragher's best friend collapsed. Carragher began to administer cardiopulmonary resuscitation. With every breath of life given, blood would squirt from a cut on the victim's lip into Carragher's mouth. His friend died of a perforated heart.

These disturbing images and memories caused Carragher to relive the traumatic events many times. He suffered from PTSD and was affected most by survivor's guilt. In 1993, he became a born-again Christian. He began studying the Bible for help from God's Word, even attending Bible college and seminary.

He received the help and the peace he had desired. Later on, after seven years of prayer and study, he wrote *Wounded Spirits* out of a desire to share that help and peace with his brothers and sisters who are still searching.

Spiritual Preparations for Your Life

To get the most from this life, you must be spiritually prepared. The essential requirement of this journey is to know Jesus as your Lord and Saviour so He can be your Guide. If you have never received Him or if you're not sure, there are four things you must understand and accept.

Recognize That You Need a Saviour

The greatest question in the Bible is, How do you find Christ? The first step in finding Christ is to recognize that you need Him, that you are a sinner, that you have violated the principles of truth in the Word of God. The Bible says in Romans 3:23, "For all have sinned, and come short of the glory of God." I have sinned and you have sinned, and because we have sinned we must have the blood of Jesus Christ cleanse us from all sin. Our morality cannot save us, our goodness cannot save us, and our acts of kindness cannot save us. Only Jesus Christ can save us.

Repent and Confess Your Sin

The Bible says in I John 1:9, "If we confess our sins, he is faithful and just to forgive us our sins, and to cleanse us from all unrighteousness." Now you might be thinking that you are not good enough. I want you to know that God can save to the uttermost. It does not matter what you have done; He can and will save you. God loves us even though we are sinners.

The Bible says in Romans 5:8, "But God commendeth his love toward us, in that, while we were yet sinners, Christ died for us." God has made it possible through His Son for you to be saved. That provision is God's gift. The Bible says in Romans 6:23, "For the wages of sin is death; but the gift of God is eternal life through Jesus Christ our Lord." For it is by grace that you have been saved through faith. It is not of yourself; it is the gift of God that you have been saved, not by works so that no one can boast.

So you see, you cannot get to Heaven by being good or by doing good works or acts of kindness. You only get to Heaven because you have confessed your sins. There must be the repentance of sin, which means you must turn away from your sins. The Bible says in Mark 1:15, "The kingdom of God is at hand: repent ye, and believe the gospel."

"Repent" means to turn away, walk and go another way.

The Gospel: the death, burial and resurrection of Jesus Christ.

If you confess with your mouth to our Lord Jesus and if you believe in your heart that God raised Jesus from the dead, you will be saved. For it is with your heart that you believe and are justified and with your mouth that you confess your sin and are saved. The result is eternal salvation, for the Bible says in Romans 10:13, "For whosoever shall call upon the name of the Lord shall be saved."

The Bible says that salvation is found in no other name given among men under Heaven—that is, none other than the name of our Lord Jesus Christ. So if you want to find Christ, all you have to do is pray this prayer. But the words themselves will not save you. Only faith in Jesus Christ can provide salvation!

A Sinner's Prayer for Eternal Salvation

What Is the Sinner's Prayer?

The sinner's prayer is a Christian term for a prayer that is said when someone wants to repent of his sin, ask God for forgiveness and state belief in the death, burial and saving resurrection of Jesus Christ. Romans 10:9 and 10 says,

> *"That if thou shalt confess with thy mouth the Lord Jesus, and shalt believe in thine heart that God hath raised him from the dead, thou shalt be saved.*
>
> *"For with the heart man believeth unto righteousness; and with the mouth confession is made unto salvation."*

Millions have come to a saving relationship with

Jesus Christ through church services, friends and family leading them in a salvation prayer. However, it is not words in a prayer that save. Jesus Christ alone has the power to save through faith. Understand that it's not the prayer that saves; it's the repentance and faith behind the prayer that lays hold of salvation.

Sample Prayer

While meaning it in your heart say a prayer like this:

> Lord Jesus Christ, I confess that I'm a sinner. I ask You to forgive me of my sins and to cleanse me of all unrighteousness. I believe that You died in my place, to pay the penalty for my sin, and rose again for my salvation. I want to turn from my sinful ways, so I now ask You, Lord Jesus, to come into my life as my Saviour and my Lord. I will serve You and obey You. I will read Your Word and I will follow Christ from this day forward all the days of my life. In Jesus' name I pray. Amen.

Now with your faith in Jesus Christ you have stepped from darkness into the light.

The difficulties of living as a Christian in a sinful world are many. Therefore, it is important that you seek other Christians to help you sustain your resolve. Go to church as often as you can to help you support your beliefs. Contact us at afbmissions.com, asking us to recommend a pastor and local church in your area. It is the Lord's will for your journey.

If you have prayed this prayer in sincere faith, you may want to put your initials by the prayer along with today's date as a reminder that you have come to Christ in faith, trusting Him as your Lord and Saviour.

1 Definitions and Thoughts

"The spirit of a man will sustain his infirmity; but a wounded spirit who can bear?"—Proverbs 18:14.

The American Psychiatric Association defines post traumatic stress disorder (PTSD) as "an anxiety (emotional) disorder which stems from a particular incident evoking significant stress."[1]

PTSD is found in survivors of combat, combat training accidents, the Holocaust, automobile accidents, sexual assaults, and other traumatic experiences.

Most survivors of trauma return to normal given a little time. However, some people have stress reactions that don't go away on their own or even get worse with time. These individuals may suffer from PTSD.[2]

PTSD is a contemporary name for an ancient disease. Whenever wars or traumatic events have occurred, they

---

1 Steve Bentley, "A Short History of PTSD," *VVA Veteran*, March/April 2005, http://www.vva.org/archive/TheVeteran/2005_03/feature_HistoryPTSD.htm (accessed January 31, 2014).

2 "Understanding and Coping With PTSD," Veterans Healthcare Administration, National Center for PTSD, January 2011, http://www.nami.org (accessed January 31, 2014).

have always had a psychological impact on people. PTSD may affect a person within a few months of a traumatic event or may appear many years later.[3]

History records many instances of PTSD. A man named Hori, a combat veteran from three thousand years ago, wrote in graphic detail about his feelings at the moment when his combat was about to begin: "You determine to go forward…Shuddering seizes you, the hair on your head stands on end, your soul lies in your hand."[4] Memories like these are real and in many cases are the cause of PTSD.

Throughout history there have been examples of warriors' dealing with tremendous fear in the face of imminent battle. During World War II, Private First Class Albert Blithe of Easy Company, 2nd Battalion, 506th Parachute Regiment, in the 101st Airborne Division, was stricken with a temporary case of hysterical blindness following days of fierce fighting to capture a stronghold in Normandy as his unit was on the way to reclaim Paris. Private Blithe recovered from the blindness and other wounds sustained in battles,[5] but he drank every day of his life.[6]

For those of you who have faced the unimaginable in standing strong and answering the call of your

---

[3] "PTSD: A Growing Epidemic," NIH *MedlinePlus*, Winter 2009, http://www.nlm.nih.gov (accessed January 31, 2014).
[4] Steve Bentley, "A Short History of PTSD," *VVA Veteran*, March/April 2005, http://www.vva.org/archive/TheVeteran/2005_03/feature_HistoryPTSD.htm (accessed January 31, 2014).
[5] "Albert Blithe," http://en.wikipedia.org (accessed January 31, 2014).
[6] Marcus Brotherton, *A Company of Heroes* (New York: Berkeley Caliber, 2010), Part 1, Chapter 1, http://books.google.com.

nation, my hope is that you will find in our Lord's Word how to be whole and fulfill the Lord's will for your life.

The renowned psychiatrist Viktor Frankl survived being imprisoned in four different Nazi concentration camps during World War II. In his book *Man's Search for Meaning,* he describes PTSD when he says that "an abnormal response to an abnormal situation is normal behavior."[7] In other words, these horrendous events will take a toll on those who endure them. In a way, these situations are part of who we are, and we cannot change them. However, we can change their effects on us.

Though I do believe Dr. Frankl is right about all our experiences being part of who we are, I know our Lord can change how we deal with the horrendous events of the past and by His grace replace our negative responses with biblical answers.

PTSD is identified by clear physical and psychological symptoms:[8]

- suicidal tendencies
- fear, depression, sleeplessness, and anxiety
- guilt and survivor's guilt
- anger and irritability
- nightmares and flashbacks
- avoidance of conflict
- apathy[9]

---

[7] Viktor E. Frankl, *Man's Search for Meaning* (New York: Touchstone, 1984), 32.
[8] David L. Conroy, "Why Is It So Hard for Us to Recover From Being Suicidal?" http://www.metanoia,org/suicide/ptsd.htm (accessed January 31, 2014); Melinda Smith, Robert Segal, and Jeanne Segal, "Post-Traumatic Stress Disorder (PTSD) Symptoms, Treatment, and Self-Help," American Academy of Experts in Traumatic Stress, http://www.aaets.org/article194.htm (accessed January 31, 2014).
[9] Lloyd Sederer, "The Enemy Is Apathy," *Psychiatric Times,* July 26, 2012, http://www.psychiatrictimes.com/blogs (accessed January 31, 2014).

It's my experience that this disorder is often associated with difficulties in social or family life, including occupational instability, marital problems, family discord, and difficulties in parenting. My research has identified more than two hundred symptoms and adverse effects. Obviously, people suffering from PTSD need help.

Many people suffering with PTSD are receiving medical treatment. This book is not meant as a replacement for that medical treatment but rather as a supplement to work in conjunction with your doctors to provide spiritual care. Though I am convinced in most cases PTSD sufferers will find great help in God's Word, you should continue to receive medical care until released by your medical professional.

The following precepts have guided me in the writing of this book.

First, I am certain that **PTSD is real** and can lead ordinary people to make rash decisions and to act inappropriately. I have known wonderful, seemingly stable people who have attempted suicide. When they are asked why, the usual answer is something like "I can't sleep" or "The battle revisits me." Another answer I heard just the other day was "They are conspiring against me," meaning that this person thought his family and friends were working behind his back to hurt him in some way when really the opposite was true. PTSD can make right seem wrong and turn lives upside down. Many have told me they fear an intervention more than a root canal or major surgery.

Many suffer from PTSD. Statistics provided by the Nebraska Department of Veterans' Affairs are staggering:[10]

- Some 7.8 percent of Americans will experience PTSD at some point in their lifetime.
- Women are twice as likely as men to suffer from PTSD.
- About 3.7 percent of U.S. adults suffer from PTSD at any given time.
- Around 30 percent of the men and women who have spent time in a war zone suffer from PTSD.
- More than half of all Vietnam veterans suffer from PTSD.

Next, **PTSD can show up at any time.** Some experts say the symptoms may first appear the day after the traumatic experience or up to many years later. A trigger, sometimes something as simple as a small noise, a wounded warriors television commercial, or a scream, can set off a chain of memories or cause pain. Many patients experience no symptoms for years—until the trigger activates them.

Obviously, we need to act and treat the afflicted as soon as we can. But it would be even better to prepare people prior to their facing traumatic experiences.

PTSD affects people of every class and status in life. Vietnam veterans, however, seem to be particularly susceptible. A medical study identified the following risk factors for the development of PTSD in a sample of Vietnam veterans that included 68 women and 414 men, of whom 88 were white, 63 black, 80

---

10 "What Is PTSD?" Nebraska Department of Veterans' Affairs, http://www.ptsd.ne.gov (accessed January 31, 2014).

Hispanic, 90 native Hawaiian, and 93 Japanese American.[11] Pre-military factors included Hispanics coming from an unstable family, being punished severely during childhood, childhood asocial behavior, and suffering from depression. The military factors were war-zone exposure and depression. Finally, recent stressful life events, post-Vietnam trauma, and depression were identified as post-military factors.

The researchers also identified certain pre-military protective factors, such as Japanese-American ethnicity, high school diploma or college education, older age at entry to war, higher socioeconomic status, and a more positive paternal relationship. Post-military protective factors included social support at homecoming and current social support.[12] Other research also indicates the protective effects of social support in averting PTSD or facilitating recovery if it develops.[13]

Another study by doctors found early intervention to be a critical preventive measure. Albert Glass and Franklin Jones concluded:

> PTSD symptoms can follow any serious psychological trauma, such as exposure to combat, accidents, torture, disasters, criminal assault and exposure to atrocities or to the sequelae of such extraordinary events. Prisoners of

---

[11] P. Schnurr, C. Lunney, and A. Sengupta. "Risk Factors for the Development Versus Maintenance of Posttraumatic Stress Disorder," *Journal of Trauma Stress 17,* no. 2 (2004); 85–95.

[12] Jennifer L. Price, "Findings From the National Vietnam Veterans' Readjustment Study," factsheet from the National Center for PTSD, United States Department of Veterans Affairs.

[13] C. Brewin, B. Andrews, and J. Valentine. "Meta-Analysis of Risk Factors for Posttraumatic Stress Disorder in Trauma-Exposed Adults," *Journal of Consulting and Clinic Psychology* 68 (October 2000): 748–66; E. Ozer, S. Best, T. Lipsey, and D. Weiss. "Predictors of Posttraumatic Stress Disorder and Symptoms in Adults: A Meta-Analysis," *Psychological Bulletin* 129 (January 2003): 52–73.

> war exposed to harsh treatment are particularly prone to develop PTSD. In their acute presentation these symptoms...include subsets of a large variety of affective, cognitive, perceptional, emotional and behavioral responses which are relatively normal responses to gross psychological trauma. If persistent, however, they develop a life of their own and may be maintained by inadvertent reinforcement. Early intervention and later avoidance of positive reinforcement (which may be subtle) for such symptoms is a critical preventive measure.[14]

Studies have shown that those prepared for the potential of a traumatic experience are more prepared to deal with the stress of a traumatic experience and therefore less likely to develop PTSD.[15]

PTSD is a disorder that is treatable and, with the Lord's help, curable. I am certain that people who develop PTSD can recover from it and live a normal happy life. Furthermore, there is an excellent chance that it can be prevented altogether when there is treatment prior to its onset. It is a good idea for all people who have had traumatic experiences to study this book and join a local PTSD Bible support group for help. In the introduction of this book, there is information about how to find a therapy group.

Personal Group Follow-Up

Memory Verse

"The spirit of a man will sustain his infirmity; but a

---

[14] Albert Julius Glass and Franklin D. Jones, *Psychiatry in the U.S. Army: Lessons for Community* (Bethesda, MD: Uniformed Services University of the Health Sciences, F. Edward Herbert School of Medicine, 2005), 26.

[15] Babette Rothschild, *The Body Remembers: The Psychophysiology of Trauma and Trauma Treatment* (New York: W. W. Norton & Company, 2000).

wounded spirit who can bear?"—Proverbs 18:14.

Discussion Points

1. What is PTSD an abnormal response to?

2. What type of event does PTSD usually follow?

3. What are some common symptoms of PTSD?

4. What category of people suffer from PTSD?

5. Is PTSD treatable?

2 The Bible on Suicide

"For ye are bought with a price: therefore glorify God in your body, and in your spirit, which are God's."—I Corinthians 6:20.

Bible Preparation

"Know ye not that ye are the temple of God, and that the Spirit of God dwelleth in you?

"If any man defile the temple of God, him shall God destroy; for the temple of God is holy, which temple ye are."—I Corinthians 3:16, 17.

"Be not over much wicked, neither be thou foolish: why shouldest thou die before thy time?"—Ecclesiastes 7:17.

"The righteous cry, and the LORD *heareth, and delivereth them out of all their troubles.*

"The LORD *is nigh unto them that are of a broken heart; and saveth such as be of a contrite spirit.*

"Many are the afflictions of the righteous: but the LORD *delivereth him out of them all.*

"He keepeth all his bones: not one of them is broken."—Psalm 34:17–20.

"What? know ye not that your body is the temple of the Holy Ghost which is in you, which ye have of God, and ye are not your own?

"For ye are bought with a price: therefore glorify God in your body, and in your spirit, which are God's."—I Corinthians 6:19, 20.

"For I know the thoughts that I think toward you, saith the LORD, thoughts of peace, and not of evil, to give you an expected end."—Jeremiah 29:11.

"And he said unto me, My grace is sufficient for thee: for my strength is made perfect in weakness. Most gladly therefore will I rather glory in my infirmities, that the power of Christ may rest upon me."—II Corinthians 12:9.

"If any man defile the temple of God, him shall God destroy; for the temple of God is holy, which temple ye are."—I Corinthians 3:17.

"I call heaven and earth to record this day against you, that I have set before you life and death, blessing and cursing: therefore choose life, that both thou and thy seed may live."—Deuteronomy 30:19.

"And I give unto them eternal life; and they shall never perish, neither shall any man pluck them out of my hand."—John 10:28.

To my way of thinking, suicide is a permanent solution to a temporary problem. If you are considering suicide as you peruse this book, I beg you to read this chapter and see the Lord's plan for your life. Also, contact a healthcare professional, the pastor of a local Bible-believing church, or a Christian counselor and seek immediate help. It is not the Lord's will for anyone to commit suicide.

As an ordained minister traveling to many churches every year and having dozens of face-to-face conversations, I have found that a month does not go by without someone's asking me questions regarding my beliefs about suicide. To answer those questions I always refer to God's never-changing Word.

So what does the Bible say about suicide? Using a topical index to research the words *suicide* and *homicide,* you can easily find instances where the Bible mentions suicides. There are at least six suicides recorded in Scripture.

The first thing we must recognize is that suicide is sin and that God hates sin. Furthermore, we never sin without hurting God and those around us whom we love. The Bible teaches that we are all sinners: "For all have sinned, and come short of the glory of God" (Romans 3:23). This means all people are sinners and do not deserve to go to Heaven.

Now we can see that we are all sinners and no sin is beyond our evil thoughts. Suicide is a sin, and as sinners we are susceptible to any sin.

As finite human beings we tend to categorize or rate our sins. In other words, we may say a little lie is more acceptable than, let's say, murder. However, in God's view all sin is the same. No sin has a greater or lesser value. Each one separates us from a relationship with God. Sin separates us from a wonderful relationship, a relationship that fills a void in our lives—the void that only the Lord can fill.

Now let's review the story of Judas Iscariot. As one of Jesus' original disciples, he was the treasurer for the group (John 13:29) but was known as a penny pincher and a thief (John 12:4–6). Also, he is notorious for kissing Jesus on the cheek and betraying Him into the hands of Sanhedrin priests in exchange for a payment of thirty pieces of silver (Matthew 26:14, 47; Mark 14:10, 42; Luke 22:1–6, 47; John 13:18; 18:2–5).

After betraying Christ, Judas suffered from great guilt. Feeling remorse, he even tried to return the money he had been paid. The Sanhedrin said it was not their problem. Judas then went out and hanged himself (Matthew 27:3–5; Acts 1:18).

The betrayal was no surprise to Jesus, and He had already identified Judas as a "devil" (John 6:70, 71). Clearly Jesus knew beforehand what the future held for Him. Nevertheless, Jesus also made it clear that He had chosen Judas to be in His group of disciples just as He had chosen the other eleven. This goes to show that it was all part of God's plan.

Satan never conspires against Jesus without Jesus' knowing. In fact, nothing happens at all unless God either causes it or allows it.

To substantiate this point, we see that Judas' act of betrayal was foretold in the Old Testament. The apostle Peter, as recorded in Acts 1:16 and 17, said that David had prophesied about Judas Iscariot many years earlier:

> *"Men and brethren, this scripture must needs have been fulfilled, which the Holy Ghost by the mouth of David spake before concerning Judas, which was guide to them that took Jesus.*
>
> *"For he was numbered with us, and had obtained part of this ministry."*

How did this happen? We're told that Satan entered Judas' heart and 'put it into his heart' to betray Jesus (John 13:2, 27). Even though this is true, we must remember that Judas had a choice. The Bible tells us that everyone is tempted and that temptation can give birth to sin (James 1:14, 15).

Satan placed in Judas' heart an idea that appealed to Judas' selfish motives. Judas' heart or spiritual condition was unprotected, and this opened the door to Satan.

What biblical evidence do we have that shows the condition of Judas' heart? In John 12, we have the wonderful account of how Mary (the sister of Lazarus, whom Jesus had raised from the dead), in an act of worship, poured expensive ointment on Jesus' feet. In that day after cleaning a person's feet, wealthy people would use ointment to heal the feet and make them smell better.

However, instead of recognizing this act for the worship it was, Judas reacted in a way that revealed a lot about his heart's condition.

> *"Then took Mary a pound of ointment of spikenard,*

very costly, and anointed the feet of Jesus, and wiped his feet with her hair: and the house was filled with the odour of the ointment.

"Then saith one of his disciples, Judas Iscariot, Simon's son, which should betray him,

"Why was not this ointment sold for three hundred pence, and given to the poor?

"This he said, not that he cared for the poor; but because he was a thief, and had the bag, and bare what was put therein."—John 12:3–6.

We see that Judas' question and the explanation that followed show us that Judas' heart was not one that had been changed by the love of Jesus. Judas was a man who had his own agenda, ideas and personal motives. Without question, he was not a man who loved God with all his heart, soul, mind, body, and strength.

You see, my dear friends, the tragedy here is that Judas' life was one of missed opportunities. He was committed to trying to solve his own problems and living life the way he wanted to. This made him so miserable that he accepted Satan's agenda for his life. Because of that, he committed suicide. The connection is clear for us. God has a plan for our lives, and it does not include suicide.

Further study on the subject of suicide brings us to what Jesus said about killing:

"Ye have heard that it was said by them of old time, Thou shalt not kill; and whosoever shall kill shall be in danger of the judgment:

"But I say unto you, That whosoever is angry with his brother without a cause shall be in danger of the judgment: and whosoever shall say to his brother, Raca, shall be in danger of the council: but whosoever shall say, Thou fool, shall be in danger of hell fire."—Matthew 5:21, 22.

Please allow me to clarify that the word "kill" in this verse means murder and in no way applies to killing to protect one's country or to ensure one's personal safety. In this passage, you can see that suicide is murder and is never the Lord's plan for any of us. If Satan places that idea in our heads, we need only to replace it with the Lord's Word.

The Lord has plans and goals for your life. You will never experience a truly happy life until you allow Him His place in your heart. From experience I can tell you that life made sense to me for the first time only after I gave myself to Him.

At the beginning of this chapter, I showed how suicide was sin and sin would separate us from the Lord and our home in Heaven.

Allow me briefly to review the Lord's plan for salvation and how to get to Heaven.

If you desire Heaven to be your final home and want the Lord to be your master, there are several steps you must take.

First, you must understand that you are a sinner. The Bible states, "For all have sinned, and come short of the glory of God" (Romans 3:23). All people are sinners and do not deserve to go to Heaven.

Second, you must realize that your sin has deadly consequences. Romans 6:23 says, "For the wages of sin is death." Here "death" refers to an eternal separation from God in Hell.

Third, you need to recognize that your sin debt has been paid. The Bible states, "But God commendeth his love toward us, in that, while we were yet sinners, Christ died for us" (Romans 5:8). Jesus Christ, the Son of God, took your punishment when He died for you!

Fourth, you must repent of your sins. "God...now commandeth all men every where to repent" (Acts 17:30). Repentance is a change of heart that causes you to turn toward God and away from your present way of life.

Finally, you must take action to ensure the Lord knows your intentions.

> *"If thou shalt confess with thy mouth the Lord Jesus, and shalt believe in thine heart that God hath raised him from the dead, thou shalt be saved.*
>
> *"For with the heart man believeth unto righteousness; and with the mouth confession is made unto salvation."*—Romans 10:9, 10.

This passage lists two aspects of salvation. You are required to confess that Jesus is Lord and also to believe in your heart that God resurrected Him. Until you do these two things, you are still on your way to Hell.

When you agreed to serve your country, community or family, you believed the promises made to you by the recruiter or partner, and you acted on those promises. To become a Christian, you must believe God's promises and act on them by asking Him to save you. God cannot lie! Here is His promise to you: "He that believeth on the Son hath everlasting life: and he that believeth not the Son shall not see life; but the wrath of God abideth on him" (John 3:36).

If you will accept Jesus Christ as your Saviour, please pray this prayer or one similar to it:

> Lord Jesus, I admit I am a sinner going to Hell. I know that I cannot save myself. I repent of my sins and put my faith in the blood that You shed for me on the cross to pay for all my sins. I now accept You as my Saviour and trust You to take me to Heaven. Thank You for saving me. Amen.

If you prayed for Christ to save you and meant it in your heart, you're saved. However, if you didn't say that prayer or did not mean it in your heart, I pray that as you go through this book or think about this over the next couple of days, the Lord will prompt you to make things right.

Personal and Group Follow-Up

Memory Verse

"For ye are bought with a price: therefore glorify God in your body, and in your spirit, which are God's."— I Corinthians 6:20.

Discussion Points

1. What type of solution is suicide?

____

____

____

____

2. Who has sinned?______________________

3. Does God categorize sins? ______________

4. What does the Lord say suicide is?

____

5. Why was Judas suicidal?

____

6. When the Lord uses the word "kill" in Matthew 5:21, what does it mean?

____

7. Why did Judas commit suicide?

____

8. Have you ever considered suicide? __________

9. Are you still considering suicide?__________

If you answered that question yes, please call a healthcare professional by dialing 911. In the meantime, seek out a family member or friend for immediate help.

10. What was the number one lesson you learned from reading this chapter?

____

____

____

____

____

____

3 The Bible on Fear and Anxiety

"For God hath not given us the spirit of fear; but of power, and of love, and of a sound mind."—II Timothy 1:7.

Bible Preparation

"Fear thou not; for I am with thee: be not dismayed; for I am thy God: I will strengthen thee; yea, I will help thee; yea, I will uphold thee with the right hand of my righteousness."—Isaiah 41:10.

"Be careful for nothing; but in every thing by prayer and supplication with thanksgiving let your requests be made known unto God.

"And the peace of God, which passeth all understanding, shall keep your hearts and minds through Christ Jesus."—Philippians 4:6, 7.

"What time I am afraid, I will trust in thee."—Psalm 56:3.

"For God hath not given us the spirit of fear; but of power, and of love, and of a sound mind."—II Timothy 1:7.

"Be strong and of a good courage, fear not, nor be afraid of them: for the LORD *thy God, he it is that doth go with thee; he will not fail thee, nor forsake thee."*—Deuteronomy 31:6.

"I sought the LORD*, and he heard me, and delivered me from all my fears."*—Psalm 34:4.

"Casting all your care upon him; for he careth for you."—I Peter 5:7.

"There is no fear in love; but perfect love casteth out fear: because fear hath torment. He that feareth is not made perfect in love."—I John 4:18.

"Have not I commanded thee? Be strong and of a good courage; be not afraid, neither be thou dismayed: for the LORD *thy God is with thee whithersoever thou goest."*—Joshua 1:9.

"Say to them that are of a fearful heart, Be strong, fear not: behold, your God will come with vengeance, even God with a recompence; he will come and save you."—Isaiah 35:4.

"Peace I leave with you, my peace I give unto you: not as the world giveth, give I unto you. Let not your heart be troubled, neither let it be afraid."—John 14:27.

"Heaviness in the heart of man maketh it stoop: but a good word maketh it glad."—Proverbs 12:25.

"Yea, though I walk through the valley of the shadow of death, I will fear no evil: for thou art with me; thy rod and thy staff they comfort me."—Psalm 23:4.

"Take therefore no thought for the morrow: for the morrow shall take thought for the things of itself. Sufficient unto the day is the evil thereof."—Matthew 6:34.

"The LORD is my light and my salvation; whom shall I fear? the LORD is the strength of my life; of whom shall I be afraid?"—Psalm 27:1.

"The LORD shall fight for you, and ye shall hold your peace."—Exodus 14:14.

In Franklin Delano Roosevelt's first inaugural address, he gave Americans one of the greatest quotes in the history of our nation: "The only thing we have to fear is fear itself."[16]

In the midst of the greatest depression this country has ever faced, the president stated our biggest enemy was fear. Notice he didn't say our biggest fear is where our next paycheck or our next meal is coming from. He didn't even mention the banks or stocks, which were in terrible shape at that time. He cut to the chase and said our greatest fear is fear.

Duke University Medical Center research links fear and anxiety with depression and sleeplessness. It seems fear brings on anxiety and then in most cases manifests itself in depression.[17] Doctors have discovered that in some cases heart muscle is actually destroyed when people are subjected to intense fear.[18]

In most cases, stress is brought on by anxiety and fear. The medical community has long warned patients

---

[16] Franklin D. Roosevelt, inaugural address of March 4, 1933, in Samuel Rosenman, ed., *The Public Papers of Franklin D. Roosevelt: The Year of Crisis, 1933* (New York: Random House, 1938), 2:11–16.
[17] Duke Medicine News and Communications, "PTSD Linked to Smaller Brain Area Regulating Fear Response," www.dukehealth.org (accessed February 1, 2014).
[18] Marilyn Cebelin and Charles Hirsch, "Human Stress Cardiomyopathy," *Human Pathology* 11 (March 1980), 123–32.

that stress caused by fear increases our risk of infectious diseases. Literally, fear causes stress, which can make us sick and even kill us.[19] We must seek the Lord's help and allow Him to defeat our fears.

Stress-causing fear is one of the greatest concerns of people facing PTSD. Often the fear is a symptom brought on by the traumas and abuse experienced previously in one's life. In other words, an individual who was shot by an enemy soldier of a certain color with certain features may fear people with those features for the rest of his life.

A young lady in the military who had been raped by a superior officer told me that for years she was uneasy around loud, forceful leaders who reminded her of the rapist. She suffered from fear, anxiety and depression. Providentially, the Lord showed her that her attacker was still, in a way, attacking her and having control over her life. She read her Bible and prayed daily for the Lord to help and was delivered. Later, after she had been healed, I attended her wedding and promotion as a high-ranking officer.

Unlike this woman, some who have experienced trauma lose faith and feel abandoned by God. Individuals with PTSD can become so preoccupied with events in the past that it can be hard for them to imagine a future.

It's common to experience feelings of anxiety following the loss of a loved one or a traumatic event.

---

[19] Ingrid Koo, "Sick of Stress or Sick From Stress?" www.About.com (accessed February 1, 2014).

Sometimes in the aftermath of an overwhelming, tragic or terrifying event, people experience not only fear but also anxiety symptoms that are severe enough to disrupt their daily routine.

I've found that PTSD can be triggered by a range of events including exposure to rape, mugging, terrorism, domestic violence, or psychological abuse. Though PTSD is common among military and law enforcement personnel, it can affect people in all walks of life.

In some cases, the atmosphere found in the PTSD treatment community is rushed and often skeptical. I talked with one doctor who believes many of the folks making PTSD claims are faking in order to get disability payments. When pressed, he mentioned that he just cannot believe the crazy type of fears seen in healthy young adults.

After going through traumatic events, you may feel like you've been abandoned by God, but this isn't the case. Beginning or strengthening your relationship with God and attending a Christian group will help you gain the strength to move forward with your life.

The Lord certainly never abandons His children. In Luke 21:26, the Lord teaches that "men's hearts [will be] failing them for fear, and for looking after those things which are coming on the earth: for the powers of heaven shall be shaken." Fear is real, and thankfully our Lord understands that.

The Bible teaches, "There is no fear in love; but perfect love casteth out fear: because fear hath torment. He that feareth is not made perfect in love" (I John 4:18).

The crux of this text is clear—we must accept the Lord's love. If we don't, we are standing in the way of our own happiness and the Lord's will for our lives.

It's sad that the implications are greater than just our own failure to enjoy the Lord's perfect love. We learn from Scripture that we sometimes get in the way of those we love, keeping them from experiencing the Lord's perfect love (I Corinthians 8:9). I know most of us care about our family and friends more than we do ourselves. We have to bite the bullet and give our lives and fears to God.

So where do we go from here? Let's closely review how the Lord's Word deals with fear.

"God hath not given us the spirit of fear; but of power, and of love, and of a sound mind" (II Timothy 1:7). It's important to realize that fear does not come from our Lord but from the Devil and those he uses in this world. God is the opposite of fear; He is hope: "Fear thou not; for I am with thee: be not dismayed; for I am thy God: I will strengthen thee; yea, I will help thee; yea, I will uphold thee with the right hand of my righteousness" (Isaiah 41:10).

God is always with us and can handle any of our fears and problems. Even through our greatest trials, the Lord is with us.

> *"What time I am afraid, I will trust in thee.*
>
> *"In God I will praise his word, in God I have put my trust; I will not fear what flesh can do unto me."*—Psalm 56:3, 4.

The secret to overcoming fear and anxiety is to trust the Lord and give Him our fears.

Over and over again, the Lord shows us that the answer is found in Him. So our choice is simple: we can trust the Lord, or we can continue to follow the Devil's plan for our lives.

In James 2:19, we read, "Thou believest that there is one God; thou doest well: the devils also believe, and tremble."

In summary, you can see that suffering from PTSD with fear and anxiety symptoms is exactly what the Devil wants us to be doing. Remember, he is the author of confusion, hatred, broken relationships, torn-apart families, and so on. The great news as seen in James 2:19 is that demons know the Lord's power and fear Him.

My friends, the victory is yours to choose. As I said at the end of the last chapter, it begins with accepting Christ as your Lord and Saviour.

If you desire to be free from fear and anxiety and to have Heaven as your final home, there are several steps you must follow.

First, you must understand that you are a sinner. The Bible states, "For all have sinned, and come short of the glory of God" (Romans 3:23). All people are sinners and do not deserve to go to Heaven.

Second, you must realize that your sin has deadly consequences. Romans 6:23 says, "For the wages of sin is death." Here "death" refers to an eternal separation from God in Hell.

Third, you need to recognize that your sin debt has been paid. The Bible states, "But God commendeth his love toward us, in that, while we were yet sinners, Christ died for us" (Romans 5:8). Jesus Christ, the Son of God, took your punishment when He died for you!

Fourth, you must repent of your sins. "God…now commandeth all men every where to repent" (Acts 17:30). Repentance is a change of heart that causes you to turn toward God and away from your present way of life.

Finally, you must take action to ensure the Lord knows your intentions.

> *"If thou shalt confess with thy mouth the Lord Jesus, and shalt believe in thine heart that God hath raised him from the dead, thou shalt be saved.*
>
> *"For with the heart man believeth unto righteousness; and with the mouth confession is made unto salvation."*— Romans 10:9, 10.

This passage lists two aspects of salvation. You are required to confess that Jesus is Lord and also to believe in your heart that God resurrected Him. Until you do these two things, you are still on your way to Hell.

When you agreed to serve your country, community or family, you believed the promises made to you by the recruiter or partner, and you acted on those promises. To become a Christian, you must believe God's promises and act on them by asking Him to save you. God cannot lie! Here is His promise to you: "He that believeth on the Son hath everlasting life: and he that believeth not the Son shall not see life; but the wrath of

God abideth on him" (John 3:36).

If you will accept Jesus Christ as your Saviour, please pray this prayer or one similar to it:

> Lord Jesus, I admit I am a sinner going to Hell. I know that I cannot save myself. I repent of my sins and put my faith in the blood that You shed for me on the cross to pay for all my sins. I now accept You as my Saviour and trust You to take me to Heaven. Thank You for saving me. Amen.

If you prayed for Christ to save you and meant it in your heart, you're saved. However, if you didn't say that prayer or did not mean it in your heart, I pray that as you go through this book or think about this over the next couple of days, the Lord will prompt you to make things right.

Personal and Group Follow-Up

Memory Verses

> *"For God hath not given us the spirit of fear; but of power, and of love, and of a sound mind."*—II Timothy 1:7.

> *"What time I am afraid, I will trust in thee.*
>
> *"In God I will praise his word, in God I have put my trust; I will not fear what flesh can do unto me."*—Psalm 56:3, 4.

Discussion Points

1. What are some physical effects of fear and anxiety?

____

____

2. What is one of the greatest concerns facing people with PTSD? ______________________

3. Does the Lord ever abandon His children? _____

4. Where is the answer to PTSD found? __________

5. List three things you learned from this chapter that may help you with your life.

A.____

____

B.____

____

C.____

____

4
The Bible on Guilt and Survivor's Guilt

"Repent ye therefore, and be converted, that your sins may be blotted out, when the times of refreshing shall come from the presence of the Lord."—Acts 3:19.

Bible Preparation

"Create in me a clean heart, O God; and renew a right spirit within me."—Psalm 51:10.

"If the Son therefore shall make you free, ye shall be free indeed."—John 8:36.

"If we confess our sins, he is faithful and just to forgive us our sins, and to cleanse us from all unrighteousness."—I John 1:9.

"There is no fear in love; but perfect love casteth out fear: because fear hath torment. He that feareth is not made perfect in love."—I John 4:18.

One of the biggest reasons so many of us are living defeated lives is guilt. In Satan's arsenal, guilt is one of his most effective weapons against us. It rips us apart.

It makes us feel dirty, unworthy and useless. It robs us of our joy and ultimately lessens our faith and confidence in our Lord.

Jesus came not only to cleanse us from our sins but also to set us free from the guilt of our sins. If you want to live a life of spiritual victory, you need to have a conscience freed from the guilt of your past. The Bible talks about "holding the mystery of the faith in a pure conscience" (I Timothy 3:9).

A quick look at my concordance shows me that guilt can be placed in one of two biblical categories. First, there's godly sorrow that leads a person to repentance (II Corinthians 7:10). This literally means to have sincere regret or remorse and to trust the Lord to cleanse your guilt. Remember, all who turn away from their sins and turn to God in genuine repentance and faith will be saved. This is conviction, which comes from the Holy Spirit (John 16:8). The Bible teaches that once a person repents of the sin in his life, the guilt lifts and he feels relieved and joyful that his sins have been forgiven.

As Oswald Chambers wrote,

> Conviction of sin is one of the rarest things that ever strikes a man. It is the threshold of an understanding of God. Jesus Christ said that when the Holy Spirit came He would convict of sin; and when the Holy Spirit rouses the conscience and brings him into the presence of God, it is not his relationship with men that bothers him, but his relationship with God.[20]

---

[20] Oswald Chambers, *My Utmost for His Highest* (Uhrichsville, OH: Barbour, 2000), 250.

Then the other kind of guilt is condemnation or accusations from the Devil. The Devil loves to torment us by reminding us about our past and continually holding our sins before us even after those sins have been forgiven. This is condemnation, and no good comes out of it whatsoever. It just tears us down, makes us feel dirty and unworthy, and robs us of our faith and confidence in our Lord. It's a lie from Hell, and it must be ignored. This is the guilt we have when we lose the soldier next to us on the battlefield or a friend dies in an accident we're involved in. The Devil will use anything in his arsenal to remind us about what happened and force us to relive the trauma. The good news is that if we are saved, the Lord will take away our guilt and give us peace.

When dealing with guilt due to a loss, we need to remember, as Paul said, that the Lord has appointed a time for us to live and a time to die (Acts 17:25, 26). The time of our death is beyond any of us and out of our hands. It was planned before the beginning of the world.

Let me take a little space to explain the difference between condemnation and conviction.

Condemnation comes from Satan and is meant to tear you down and ruin your life. It points out what a failure you are and how badly you've messed up your life. It is constantly showing you the problem but never presents the solution. This is the essence of the way the Devil tries to defeat us.

The Bible teaches that with our Lord the opposite

is true. Remember, the Lord did not come to condemn the world; He came to save it (John 12:47). Also, there is no condemnation in our Lord (Romans 8:1). On the other hand, the Devil is known for condemning and accusing believers (Revelation 12:10).

You will never hear God telling you what a failure you are because Jesus said, "I came not to judge the world, but to save the world" (John 12:47). Remember, condemnation is from the Devil, and you can find relief in the Lord. I am so thankful the Lord has given me victory over condemnation.

Conviction is referred to in the Bible as godly sorrow. God's Word tells us, "...godly sorrow worketh repentance" (II Corinthians 7:10). Condemnation is designed by the Devil to tell you, "You are a failure and have nothing to offer anyone! Look at what you're doing with your life!" while the conviction of the Holy Spirit tells you, "Come to Me, and I will forgive you!"

Martin Luther once said, "My conscience is captive to the Word of God...To go against conscience is neither right nor safe."

Too often we are quick to follow people of worldly status and wealth while disregarding the Lord's Word. For years I tried to work my way to Heaven while dealing with a buildup of guilt. I was held captive by the world's lies and devices. Thankfully, I am now captive to the only One who can cleanse and forgive me of my sins.

Not only is God *willing* to forgive your sins, but He

wants to be gracious to you and have mercy on you: "Therefore will the LORD wait, that he may be gracious unto you, and therefore will he be exalted, that he may have mercy upon you: for the LORD is a God of judgment: blessed are all they that wait for him" (Isaiah 30:18).

We need to remember our Lord's words in I John 1:9: "If we confess our sins, he is faithful and just to forgive us our sins, and to cleanse us from all unrighteousness." By having our sins cleansed, we will leave our guilt behind.

It's obvious that conviction shows you the answers to your problems. Ultimately, it leads you to the blood of Jesus that washes away your sins.

The difference between conviction and condemnation is simple. Conviction gives you the answer while condemnation only shows you the problem. That is how the Devil operates, and it's all he can do.

Remember that the Devil possesses no divine attributes like our Lord. He is not omnipotent, omnipresent or omniscient; nor does he have any other heavenly attribute. He projects himself through media and people steeped in sin. The only attribute that can be credited to him is ubiquity, which simply means being found or appearing everywhere. McDonald's and Coke are found everywhere too, but I don't rely on them for advice.

Condemnation constantly reminds you about your past, your sin, your failures, your abuses, abuser(s), and your trauma. But conviction should remind you that Jesus died for your sins and provides comfort to the afflicted. I cannot help but quote Mark 5:34, "Thy faith hath made thee whole." Do you want comfort? Do you want healing? You will find them only in Jesus. He alone will heal your spirit.

We have covered how guilt can be an open door allowing tormenting by the Devil and how the Lord can heal us. Now we must cover one more step that everyone must take to achieve complete freedom from guilt and the shackles it holds us in. We need to forgive those who have hurt us.

In Matthew 18, Jesus teaches on forgiveness, telling us how important it is to forgive those who have wronged us and how if we don't forgive, we can be turned over to evil. In Colossians 3:13, Scripture tells us to forgive one another. The verse is clear—we must forgive.

One verse that drives this all home for us is II Corinthians 5:17: "Therefore if any man be in Christ, he is a new creature: old things are passed away; behold, all things are become new."

Your mission is obvious:

1. Flee from the condemnation that comes from the Devil.
2. Give your life and guilt to Christ.
3. Follow the Holy Spirit's conviction and forgive others.

If you desire to be free from guilt and to have Heaven as your final home, there are several steps you must follow.

First, you must understand that you are a sinner. The Bible states, "For all have sinned, and come short of the glory of God" (Romans 3:23). All people are sinners and do not deserve to go to Heaven.

Second, you must realize that your sin has deadly consequences. Romans 6:23 says, "For the wages of sin is death." Here "death" refers to an eternal separation from God in Hell.

Third, you need to recognize that your sin debt has been paid. The Bible states, "But God commendeth his love toward us, in that, while we were yet sinners, Christ died for us" (Romans 5:8). Jesus Christ, the Son of God, took your punishment when He died for you!

Fourth, you must repent of your sins. "God…now commandeth all men every where to repent" (Acts 17:30). Repentance is a change of heart that causes you to turn toward God and away from your present way of life.

Finally, you must take action to ensure the Lord knows your intentions.

> *"If thou shalt confess with thy mouth the Lord Jesus, and shalt believe in thine heart that God hath raised him from the dead, thou shalt be saved.*
>
> *"For with the heart man believeth unto righteousness; and with the mouth confession is made unto salvation."*—Romans 10:9, 10.

This passage lists two aspects of salvation. You are required to confess that Jesus is Lord and also to believe in your heart that God resurrected Him. Until you do these two things, you are still on your way to Hell.

When you agreed to serve your country, community or family, you believed the promises made to you by the recruiter or partner, and you acted on those promises. To become a Christian, you must believe God's promises and act on them by asking Him to save you. God cannot lie! Here is His promise to you: "He that believeth on the Son hath everlasting life: and he that believeth not the Son shall not see life; but the wrath of God abideth on him" (John 3:36).

If you will accept Jesus Christ as your Saviour, please pray this prayer or one similar to it:

> Lord Jesus, I admit I am a sinner going to Hell. I know that I cannot save myself. I repent of my sins and put my faith in the blood that You shed for me on the cross to pay for all my sins. I now accept You as my Saviour and trust You to take me to Heaven. Thank You for saving me. Amen.

If you prayed for Christ to save you and meant it in your heart, you're saved. However, if you didn't say that prayer or did not mean it in your heart, I pray that as you go through this book or think about this over the next couple of days, the Lord will prompt you to make things right.

Personal and Group Follow-Up

Memory Verses

"Repent ye therefore, and be converted, that your sins may be blotted out, when the times of refreshing shall come from the presence of the Lord."—Acts 3:19.

"Therefore if any man be in Christ, he is a new

creature: old things are passed away; behold, all things are become new."—II Corinthians 5:17.

Discussion Points

1. Who sets us free from guilt?________________

2. What are the two biblical categories of guilt?

____

____

3. What is condemnation?

____

____

____

____

4. What is conviction?

____

____

____

____

5. What lesson have you learned from this chapter that will help you?

____

____

____

____

____

____

____

____

5

The Bible on Anger and Irritability

"Be not hasty in thy spirit to be angry: for anger resteth in the bosom of fools."—Ecclesiastes 7:9.

Bible Preparation

"Wherefore, my beloved brethren, let every man be swift to hear, slow to speak, slow to wrath."—James 1:19.

"Be not hasty in thy spirit to be angry: for anger resteth in the bosom of fools."—Ecclesiastes 7:9.

"Peace I leave with you, my peace I give unto you: not as the world giveth, give I unto you. Let not your heart be troubled, neither let it be afraid."—John 14:27.

"He that is slow to anger is better than the mighty; and he that ruleth his spirit than he that taketh a city."—Proverbs 16:32.

"And the servant of the Lord must not strive; but be gentle unto all men, apt to teach, patient."—II Timothy 2:24.

"But the fruit of the Spirit is love, joy, peace, longsuffering, gentleness, goodness, faith,

"Meekness, temperance: against such there is no law."—Galatians 5:22, 23.

"Train up a child in the way he should go: and when he is old, he will not depart from it."—Proverbs 22:6.

"Be ye angry, and sin not: let not the sun go down upon your wrath:

"Neither give place to the devil."—Ephesians 4:26, 27.

"He that hath no rule over his own spirit is like a city that is broken down, and without walls."—Proverbs 25:28.

"A fool uttereth all his mind: but a wise man keepeth it in till afterwards."—Proverbs 29:11.

"And we know that all things work together for good to them that love God, to them who are the called according to his purpose."—Romans 8:28.

"Not given to wine, no striker, not greedy of filthy lucre; but patient, not a brawler, not covetous."—I Timothy 3:3.

"God is a Spirit: and they that worship him must worship him in spirit and in truth."—John 4:24.

"Anger is one letter short of danger" (Unknown).

If there is one thing I have learned in my life, it is that anger is a response to actions or pain directed against you. Think about it; it's an emotion that is always a reaction to some form of hurt. It's obvious to me that anger is reflected hurt against you.

From the time we're very young, we're trained by everything around us to respond to hurt with more hurt or what we know as anger. It's a self-protective reflex.

I've known folks who have been angry and irritable their entire lives. For them, it's a choice, a decision, an evil prompting, and unfortunately a way of life that brings no honor or glory to the Lord, not to mention that it kills wonderful relationships and destroys families.

A friend of mine who suffers from PTSD told me that the symptom that affects him daily that he most wishes he didn't have is anger. He can see it tearing apart relationships but has no idea what to do about it. In fact, anger is one of the symptoms felt most by people with PTSD.[21]

Anger is not always sin, according to the Bible. There is a type of anger that is acceptable; it is called righteous indignation. In Psalm 7:11 we see that "God judgeth the righteous, and God is angry with the wicked every day."

Mark 3:5 says, "[Jesus] looked round about on them with anger, being grieved for the hardness of their hearts." Righteous indignation is when we're upset with folks who go against our Lord's Word and design for their lives. For instance, if someone is always using the Lord's name in vain or promoting sin, it's okay for us to show righteous indignation.

The Bible teaches that anger becomes sinful when it is motivated by pride. Let's look at James 1:20: "For the wrath of man worketh not the righteousness of

---

[21] Melinda Smith, Robert Segal, and Jeanne Segal, "Post-Traumatic Stress Disorder (PTSD) Symptoms, Treatment, and Self-Help," American Academy of Experts in Traumatic Stress, http://www.aaets.org/article194.htm (accessed January 31, 2014).

God." Prideful anger is never acceptable.

The way to handle anger biblically is by recognizing and admitting as sin our prideful anger and our wrong handling of it.

In Proverbs 28:13 we read, "He that covereth his sins shall not prosper: but whoso confesseth and forsaketh them shall have mercy." It's clear we must confess and forsake our sinful anger.

I find two types of anger prevalent in the Bible—slow anger and quick anger. Slow anger is very dangerous. It's the type that gradually eats away at you and your heart and gets in the way of your testimony. The scary thing is it's so slow that others may not see it. It's easy to hide. Ephesians 4:26, 27 describes this type of anger:

> *"Be ye angry, and sin not: let not the sun go down upon your wrath:*
>
> *"Neither give place to the devil."*

These plain words speak volumes. If we continue on with besetting anger, we're giving place in our lives to the Devil.

On many occasions, I've been guilty of quick anger. I'd get mad without praying or thinking through a situation, and then I'd blow up. This type of anger is dangerous as well, and we must pray and work hard to avoid it.

The Bible teaches in Proverbs 29:11, "A fool uttereth all his mind: but a wise man keepeth it in till afterwards."

It should be the goal of every one of us to 'keep it in till afterwards.' In other words, we should slow life down a bit and carefully consider whether we should be angry.

Whether it is slow or quick anger, we must release it. We must not have anger if we want to serve our Lord in a productive manner. With that in mind, perhaps the toughest thing we learn about anger is that it has its consequences. One of my seminar professors outlined six biblical characteristics of anger. Here's my explanation of each:

1. Anger is unacceptable to God, and it will hurt your relationships with Him and with those around you. James 1:19, 20 says,

> *"Wherefore, my beloved brethren, let every man be swift to hear, slow to speak, slow to wrath:*
>
> *"For the wrath of man worketh not the righteousness of God."*

The bottom line is, we'll never accomplish God's will with anger.

2. Anger leads to more anger in a vicious cycle which culminates in the destruction of all we hold precious. Proverbs 10:12 teaches, "Hatred stirreth up strifes: but love covereth all sins." If you think your anger is bad now, just wait. You haven't seen anything yet.

3. Anger is addictive. In Proverbs 19:19, we see this truth: "A man of great wrath shall suffer punishment: for if thou deliver him, yet thou must do it again." It is a continuous evil cycle that is addictive. It's also true that angry people need to trust the Lord to break the cycle.

4. Anger leads to hostile situations and arrests. Matthew 5:25 commands, "Agree with thine adversary quickly, whiles thou art in the way with him; lest at any time the adversary deliver thee to the judge, and the judge deliver thee to the officer, and thou be cast into prison." Anger costs folks a whole lot of money. Lawyers and hospital visits are expensive.

5. Anger always necessitates reconciliation. In Matthew 5:23, 24, Jesus says,

> *"Therefore if thou bring thy gift to the altar, and there rememberest that thy brother hath ought against thee;*
>
> *"Leave there thy gift before the altar, and go thy way; first be reconciled to thy brother, and then come and offer thy gift."*

He is literally saying not to come to the altar until you get things right with your brother. The Lord expects us to resolve anger so that our relationships are such that we can worship at the altar.

6. Anger always necessitates restoration. Proverbs 14:17 is clear: "He that is soon angry dealeth foolishly: and a man of wicked devices is hated." Angry people constantly hurt other people and cause offense. You can never be free from anger until you restore the relationships hurt by anger.

It's pretty straightforward—anger has many consequences. It is a disease against spirituality and will always stand in the way of your being in the Lord's perfect will.

In order to remove anger from our lives, we must complete the following steps:

1. Accept the truth. In Galatians 5:13–26, we are taught that we are called into liberty—not hatred, idolatry, indignation, wrath (anger), or any other type of ungodly behavior.

2. Deal with your anger immediately (keep short accounts). James 1:19, 20 says,

"Wherefore, my beloved brethren, let every man be swift to hear, slow to speak, slow to wrath:

"For the wrath of man worketh not the righteousness of God."

The Bible's instruction is straight to the point: be quick to listen and very slow to get angry. Also, as we read earlier in Ephesians 4:26, we must resolve our anger before the sun goes down.

3. Replace anger with kindness. Ephesians 4:31, 32 says,

"Let all bitterness, and wrath, and anger, and clamour, and evil speaking, be put away from you, with all malice:

"And be ye kind one to another, tenderhearted, forgiving one another, even as God for Christ's sake hath forgiven you."

If we hope to succeed, we must replace anger with kindness. To have victory over PTSD, we need to give the Lord our anger.

If you desire to be free from anger and to have Heaven as your final home, there are several steps you must follow.

First, you must understand that you are a sinner. The Bible states, "For all have sinned, and come short of the glory of God" (Romans 3:23). All people are sinners and do not deserve to go to Heaven.

Second, you must realize that your sin has deadly consequences. Romans 6:23 says, "For the wages of sin is death." Here "death" refers to an eternal separation from God in Hell.

Third, you need to recognize that your sin debt has been paid. The Bible states, "But God commendeth his love toward us, in that, while we were yet sinners, Christ died for us" (Romans 5:8). Jesus Christ, the Son of God, took your punishment when He died for you!

Fourth, you must repent of your sins. "God…now commandeth all men every where to repent" (Acts 17:30). Repentance is a change of heart that causes you to turn toward God and away from your present way of life.

Finally, you must take action to ensure the Lord knows your intentions.

> *"If thou shalt confess with thy mouth the Lord Jesus, and shalt believe in thine heart that God hath raised him from the dead, thou shalt be saved.*
>
> *"For with the heart man believeth unto righteousness; and with the mouth confession is made unto salvation."*—Romans 10:9, 10.

This passage lists two aspects of salvation. You are required to confess that Jesus is Lord and also to believe in your heart that God resurrected Him. Until you do these two things, you are still on your way to Hell.

When you agreed to serve your country, community or family, you believed the promises made to you by the recruiter or partner, and you acted on those promises. To become a Christian, you must believe God's promises and act on them by asking Him to save you. God cannot lie! Here is His promise to you: "He that believeth on the Son hath everlasting life: and he that believeth not the Son shall not see life; but the wrath of God abideth on him" (John 3:36).

If you will accept Jesus Christ as your Saviour, please pray this prayer or one similar to it:

> Lord Jesus, I admit I am a sinner going to Hell. I know that I cannot save myself. I repent of my sins and put my faith in the blood that You shed for me on the cross to pay for all my sins. I now accept You as my Saviour and trust You to take me to Heaven. Thank You for saving me. Amen.

If you prayed for Christ to save you and meant it in your heart, you're saved. However, if you didn't say that prayer or did not mean it in your heart, I pray that as you go through this book or think about this over the next couple of days, the Lord will prompt you to make things right.

Personal and Group Follow-Up

Memory Verses

"Be not hasty in thy spirit to be angry: for anger resteth in the bosom of fools."—Ecclesiastes 7:9.

"Let all bitterness, and wrath, and anger, and clamour, and evil speaking, be put away from you, with all malice:

"And be ye kind one to another, tenderhearted, forgiving one another, even as God for Christ's sake hath forgiven you."—Ephesians 4:31, 32.

Discussion Points

1. What is anger a response to?

____

____

____

2. What are we taught about anger when we are children? ____________________________________

____

3. What are the two prevalent types of anger?

____and

____

4. How should we handle anger?

____

____

____

5. What should we replace anger with?

____

____

____

____

6 The Bible on Nightmares and Flashbacks

"When thou liest down, thou shalt not be afraid: yea, thou shalt lie down, and thy sleep shall be sweet."—Proverbs 3:24.

Bible Preparation

"I will both lay me down in peace, and sleep: for thou, LORD, only makest me dwell in safety."—Psalm 4:8.

"He that dwelleth in the secret place of the most High shall abide under the shadow of the Almighty.

"I will say of the LORD, He is my refuge and my fortress: my God; in him will I trust.

"Surely he shall deliver thee from the snare of the fowler, and from the noisome pestilence.

"He shall cover thee with his feathers, and under his wings shalt thou trust: his truth shall be thy shield and buckler.

"Thou shalt not be afraid for the terror by night; nor for the arrow that flieth by day."—Psalm 91:1–5.

"Submit yourselves therefore to God. Resist the devil, and he will flee from you."—James 4:7.

"For God hath not given us the spirit of fear; but of power, and of love, and of a sound mind."—II Timothy 1:7.

"The fear of the LORD *tendeth to life: and he that hath it shall abide satisfied; he shall not be visited with evil."*—Proverbs 19:23.

"When thou goest, it shall lead thee; when thou sleepest, it shall keep thee; and when thou awakest, it shall talk with thee."—Proverbs 6:22.

"Upon this I awaked, and beheld; and my sleep was sweet unto me."—Jeremiah 31:26.

"It is vain for you to rise up early, to sit up late, to eat the bread of sorrows: for so he giveth his beloved sleep."—Psalm 127:2.

"Having therefore these promises, dearly beloved, let us cleanse ourselves from all filthiness of the flesh and spirit, perfecting holiness in the fear of God."—II Corinthians 7:1.

According to the *New York Times,* about seven percent of the general population experience at least one nightmare a week.[22] Trauma survivors with PTSD are even more likely to suffer from nightmares. One study involving Vietnam veterans suggested that as many as 52 percent of combat veterans regularly suffer from nightmares. More recent PTSD research places that number much higher, with some studies reporting

[22] Tara Parker-Pope, "Rewriting Your Nightmares," *New York Times,* October 31, 2008, http://well.blogs.nytimes.com (accessed January 31, 2014).

that between 71 percent and 96 percent of those suffering from PTSD have nightmares.[23]

As we can see, a majority of the people who have PTSD suffer from nightmares. According to Dr. Meredith Sheena, such nightmares have many detrimental health effects.[24] I have several friends with PTSD, and all have mentioned they suffer from nightmares. They have told me they're afraid to sleep and as a result are tired and feel weak throughout the day. Several have suggested that the lack of sleep is the cause of other health problems. Research seems to validate their beliefs:

> Among people who experience nightmares, those who are anxious or depressed are more likely to be distressed about the experience and suffer more psychological ill effects. Nightmares have been associated with suicide although the relationship is not causal. If you experience nightmares regularly, they may have a significant impact on your quality of life. If this is the case, it's important to consult your doctor.…Sleep deprivation, which can be caused by nightmares, can contribute to causing a number of medical conditions, including heart disease, depression and obesity.[25]

What do nightmares that follow trauma look like? Such nightmares often involve the same scary elements that were in the trauma. For example, someone who went through the battle for Fallujah may have dreams about the overwhelming enemy forces or the lack of supplies. He may dream about trying to escape the

---

[23] "Nightmares and PTSD," National Center for PTSD, http://www.ptsd.va.gov/public/problems/nightmares.asp (accessed January 31, 2014).

[24] "Sleep Disorders Guide: Adult Nightmares," www.boots.webmd.com (accessed February 1, 2014).

[25] Ibid.

battle or being in a fighting position that doesn't feel safe. A survivor of a hold-up might have nightmares about the robber or about being held at gunpoint.

Not all nightmares that occur after trauma are a direct replay of the event. About half of those who have nightmares after trauma have dreams that replay the trauma, but people with PTSD are more likely to have dreams that are exact replays of the event than are survivors without PTSD.[26]

Lab research has shown that nightmares after trauma are different in some ways from nightmares in general. Nightmares after trauma may occur earlier in the night and during different stages of sleep. They are more likely to have body movements along with them.[27]

Many people with PTSD struggle with flashbacks, which are considered one of the "re-experiencing" symptoms of PTSD. In a flashback, a person may feel or act as though the traumatic event is happening again. A flashback may be temporary, and some connection with the present moment may be maintained, or a person may lose all awareness of what is going on around him and be taken completely back to his traumatic event. For example, a rape survivor, when triggered, may begin to smell certain scents or feel pain in her body similar to that which was experienced

---

[26] Ibid.

[27] L. Wittmann et. al., "Dreaming in Posttraumatic Stress Disorder: A Critical Review of Phenomenology, Psychophysiology and Treatment. *Psychotherapy and Psychosomatics* 76 (2007): 25–39.

during her assault.[28] Flashbacks are very dangerous if the person is driving, baby-sitting or leading a group.

Many people with PTSD also experience dissociation, which is an experience in which a person feels disconnected from himself and his surroundings. Similar to flashbacks, dissociation may range from temporarily losing touch with things that are going on around you (like what happens when you daydream) to having no memories for a prolonged period of time and feeling as though you are outside of your own body.[29]

Both flashbacks and dissociation may occur as a result of encountering a trigger, or a reminder of a traumatic event that took place in your life. To the extent that people are not aware of their triggers, flashbacks and dissociation can be incredibly disruptive and unpredictable events that are difficult to manage. However, you can take steps better to manage and prevent flashbacks and dissociation.[30]

In coping with flashbacks and dissociation, prevention is key. Flashbacks and dissociation are often triggered or cued by some kind of reminder of a traumatic event (for example, encountering certain people or going to specific places) or some other stressful experience. Therefore, it is important to identify the specific things

---

[28] Tina Crenshaw, "Nightmares and PTSD: Research Review," U.S. Department of Veterans Affairs, http://www.ptsd.va.gov (accessed January 3, 2014).

[29] B. Krakow et. al., "Nightmares, Insomnia, and Sleep-Disordered Breathing in Fire Evacuees Seeking Treatment for Posttraumatic Sleep Disturbance," *Journal of Traumatic Stress* 17, no. 6 (2004): 257–68.

[30] M. M. Linehan, *Skills Training Manual for Treating Borderline Personality Disorder* (New York: Guilford Press, 1993).

that trigger flashbacks or dissociation.

By knowing what your triggers are, you can either try to limit your exposure to those triggers, or if that is not possible, you can prepare for them by devising ways to manage your reactions to those triggers.[31]

In addition to its being a way to reduce flashbacks and dissociation, learning your triggers may also help with other symptoms of PTSD, such as intrusive thoughts and memories of a traumatic event.[32]

I agree with these recommendations, but I'm grateful that we have another avenue and that no PTSD symptom ever catches the Lord by surprise. He alone is the permanent answer to all the symptoms.

If you're like so many of us who have reached the point of being sick and tired of having nightmares and flashbacks, you'll be glad to know there is a way out. It is the only way out with permanent success.

The Lord invites us in Matthew 11:28, "Come unto me, all ye that labour and are heavy laden, and I will give you rest." The first step in receiving victory from our Lord is to go to Him.

The Lord also teaches us in His Word that He is the only One who gives us safe sleep (Psalm 4:8).

A few years back when I was leading a Bible study in the military district of Washington, D.C., a young

---

[31] American Psychiatric Association, *Diagnostic and Statistical Manual of Mental Disorders,* 4th ed. (Washington, D.C.: 1994).

[32] M. M. Linehan, *Skills Training Manual for Treating Borderline Personality Disorder* (New York: Guilford Press, 1993).

man complained about never sleeping and about fighting nightmares and flashbacks from Desert Storm. The young man was saved in a Bible study and then submitted to a daily study of God's Word and weekly accountability sessions. By the end of the second week, this man was nightmare free.

A prisoner whose experience was similar said, "The nightmares have stopped and I'm now having sweet dreams!"[33]

These men were tired and heavy laden when they went to Christ for help. The Lord kept His promise and was waiting with open arms (Matthew 11:28).

Consider what the Lord said to the Israelites:

> *"For I will pass through the land of Egypt this night, and will smite all the firstborn in the land of Egypt, both man and beast; and against all the gods of Egypt I will execute judgment: I am the Lord.*
>
> *"And the blood shall be to you for a token upon the houses where ye are: and when I see the blood, I will pass over you, and the plague shall not be upon you to destroy you, when I smite the land of Egypt."*—Exodus 12:12, 13.

The lesson here is helpful. The Israelites were instructed how to protect their children when the Lord was about to bring judgment on Egypt. They were told to rub the blood of a lamb on the door frames of their homes.

---

[33] Dan Delzell, "How to Say 'No' to Nightmares," *Christian Post*, November 21, 2011, http://www.christianpost.com/news/how-to-say-no-to-nightmares-62517 (accessed February 1, 2014).

The blood of that animal for the Israelites represented "the blood of the Lamb," who was Jesus Christ. John the Baptist announced the Messiah with these words: "Behold the Lamb of God, which taketh away the sin of the world" (John 1:29). His blood has the supernatural power to forgive sins and to set captives free. The blood of Jesus is powerful and effective in the realm of thoughts, behavior, addictions, and even in the realm of your subconsciousness and your dreams.[34]

Here is how you can apply Jesus' blood to your sleep. When you go to bed at night, you can pray something like this out loud:

> Lord Jesus, please protect me, my mind and my dreams with Your blood. Please protect me from any nightmares I may have. Lord, I apply the blood of Jesus to my sleep tonight and every night. Watch over me, dear Lord. I trust in You, Jesus, to forgive my sins and to protect my mind. In Your name I pray. Amen.

Please apply this every night. God wants you to experience a great night's sleep and be in His will.

In summary, the Christian life does not advance just automatically; you must work at it. Likewise, a peaceful night's rest is not automatic. It involves the active participation of the believer crying out to the Saviour for protection from those things that are not from God. Choose Jesus over nightmares.

Additionally, I've always answered daytime evil thoughts and daydreams with an arsenal of memorized Bible verses. It always works.

---

[34] Ibid.

The mission is easy with this symptom. First, minimize your exposure to triggers. Next, after being saved, protect your life with the blood of Christ. Claim it through memorizing verses and answering nightmares and dreams by claiming those verses. If you desire to be free of nightmares and flashbacks and to have Heaven as your final home, there are several steps you must follow.

First, you must understand that you are a sinner. The Bible states, "For all have sinned, and come short of the glory of God" (Romans 3:23). All people are sinners and do not deserve to go to Heaven.

Second, you must realize that your sin has deadly consequences. Romans 6:23 says, "For the wages of sin is death." Here "death" refers to an eternal separation from God in Hell.

Third, you need to recognize that your sin debt has been paid. The Bible states, "But God commendeth his love toward us, in that, while we were yet sinners, Christ died for us" (Romans 5:8). Jesus Christ, the Son of God, took your punishment when He died for you!

Fourth, you must repent of your sins. "God…now commandeth all men every where to repent" (Acts 17:30). Repentance is a change of heart that causes you to turn toward God and away from your present way of life.

Finally, you must take action to ensure the Lord knows your intentions.

"If thou shalt confess with thy mouth the Lord Jesus, and shalt believe in thine heart that God hath raised him

from the dead, thou shalt be saved.

"For with the heart man believeth unto righteousness; and with the mouth confession is made unto salvation."—Romans 10:9, 10.

This passage lists two aspects of salvation. You are required to confess that Jesus is Lord and also to believe in your heart that God resurrected Him. Until you do these two things, you are still on your way to Hell.

When you agreed to serve your country, community or family, you believed the promises made to you by the recruiter or partner, and you acted on those promises. To become a Christian, you must believe God's promises and act on them by asking Him to save you. God cannot lie! Here is His promise to you: "He that believeth on the Son hath everlasting life: and he that believeth not the Son shall not see life; but the wrath of God abideth on him" (John 3:36).

If you will accept Jesus Christ as your Saviour, please pray this prayer or one similar to it:

> Lord Jesus, I admit I am a sinner going to Hell. I know that I cannot save myself. I repent of my sins and put my faith in the blood that You shed for me on the cross to pay for all my sins. I now accept You as my Saviour and trust You to take me to Heaven. Thank You for saving me. Amen.

If you prayed for Christ to save you and meant it in your heart, you're saved. However, if you didn't say that prayer or did not mean it in your heart, I pray that as you go through this book or think about this over the next couple of days, the Lord will prompt you to make things right.

Personal and Group Follow-Up

Memory Verses

"When thou liest down, thou shalt not be afraid: yea, thou shalt lie down, and thy sleep shall be sweet."—Proverbs 3:24.

"Come unto me, all ye that labour and are heavy laden, and I will give you rest."—Matthew 11:28.

Discussion Points

1. What is the percentage of veterans with PTSD who suffer from nightmares?

____

____

2. Is it safe to say that most people who suffer from PTSD suffer from nightmares? ____________________

3. Does the Christian life advance automatically?

____

4. Name three things you learned from this lesson.

____

____

____

____

____

____

____

5. Would you like to share a testimony with the group from your study of this chapter?____________

7 The Bible on Avoiding Conflicts

"Let us therefore follow after the things which make for peace, and things wherewith one may edify another."—Romans 14:19.

Bible Preparation

"Moreover if thy brother shall trespass against thee, go and tell him his fault between thee and him alone: if he shall hear thee, thou hast gained thy brother.

"But if he will not hear thee, then take with thee one or two more, that in the mouth of two or three witnesses every word may be established.

"And if he shall neglect to hear them, tell it unto the church: but if he neglect to hear the church, let him be unto thee as an heathen man and a publican."—Matthew 18:15–17.

"Wherefore, my beloved brethren, let every man be swift to hear, slow to speak, slow to wrath."—James 1:19.

"A soft answer turneth away wrath: but grievous words stir up anger."—Proverbs 15:1.

"Blessed are the peacemakers: for they shall be called the children of God."—Matthew 5:9.

"Look not every man on his own things, but every man also on the things of others."—Philippians 2:4.

"Take heed to yourselves: If thy brother trespass against thee, rebuke him; and if he repent, forgive him.

"And if he trespass against thee seven times in a day, and seven times in a day turn again to thee, saying, I repent; thou shalt forgive him."—Luke 17:3, 4.

"Forbearing one another, and forgiving one another, if any man have a quarrel against any: even as Christ forgave you, so also do ye."—Colossians 3:13.

"When a man's ways please the LORD, *he maketh even his enemies to be at peace with him."*—Proverbs 16:7.

"Thou shalt not avenge, nor bear any grudge against the children of thy people, but thou shalt love thy neighbour as thyself: I am the LORD.*"*—Leviticus 19:18.

"Leave there thy gift before the altar, and go thy way; first be reconciled to thy brother, and then come and offer thy gift."—Matthew 5:24.

"Be ye angry, and sin not: let not the sun go down upon your wrath."

"Let all bitterness, and wrath, and anger, and clamour, and evil speaking, be put away from you, with all malice."—Ephesians 4:26, 31.

Dr. Walt Yoho, one of my seminary professors, loved to tell this story about conflict:

> There was a man who was shipwrecked on a deserted island. He was an intelligent, hard-working man; and by the time he was rescued ten years later, he had

> managed to build a beautiful little town that consisted of several buildings. The rescuers were amazed at his handiwork and asked what each building was. The man was glad to point out his accomplishments.
>
> He said, "The first building right there is my house." They marveled that it had several rooms and even had inside plumbing. The rescuers were amazed and complimented him. Then there were two other buildings.
>
> "The next building there is my church, and it even has a pulpit and pews," he said. Again, the rescuers were blown away by the workmanship. Finally, the man pointed to the last building and said, "That's the church I used to go to. We couldn't get along so I built a new church."[35]

Dr. Yoho used that story to drive home the point that no one is without conflict. We are finite human beings living in an evil world. Avoiding conflict is a byproduct of our situation. The good thing is, we have an infinite God to help us resolve our conflicts.

A couple of years ago at a church where I was preaching, I could not help but notice a young lady and a couple small kids waiting around to speak with me after most of the people had left. She must have waited about twenty minutes as I signed Bibles and passed out prayer cards. I could tell she was overwhelmed and needed advice.

She began by asking me if one symptom of PTSD is avoiding conflict and sometimes withdrawing from life. She went on to tell me that since her husband had returned home from Afghanistan, he would often get quiet and just answer all her questions with "I'm fine."

---

[35] Dr. Walter Yoho is a well-known seminary professor and author currently serving at Tabernacle Bible Baptist College and Theological Seminary in Virginia Beach, Virginia.

She went on to say, "He even quit college rather than to have to deal with other students or professors. He has become a recluse and chooses not to deal with anyone."

I told her that not only was this behavior one of the symptoms, but that so many veterans struggle with it that it made the Nebraska Department of Veterans' Affairs list of major symptoms.[36]

Unfortunately, this young wife is not unique. There are many marriages where the partner who suffers from PTSD has shut down. In most cases there is avoidance of conflict, and conflict left unresolved can eat away at a person and shut him down. Essentially, the person seems to have given up.

Even more startling is the observation by a doctor that a person who suffers from PTSD is more than twice as likely to divorce or separate from his spouse.[37] The inability to handle conflicts is a major cause of divorce.

Even with all this information, we need to realize that God created us for relationships. I know exactly what some people will say about that: "If God created us for relationships, why do we have so many problems?" It's because we let unresolved conflict rob us of the joy that healthy Christian relationships bring.

If we're going to address conflict in a Christian

---

[36] "What Is PTSD?" Nebraska Department of Veterans' Affairs, http://www.ptsd.ne.gov (accessed January 31, 2014).

[37] Dr. Joseph Calabrese, a psychiatrist at University Hospital's Case Medical Center in Cleveland, Ohio, quoted in Katie Moisse, "Army Hospital Accused of Reversing PTSD Diagnoses to Cut Costs," ABC News, March 22, 2012, abcnews.com (accessed February 1, 2014).

manner, we need to know the rules. We need to understand that conflict is inevitable. No relationship of any type is immune. But when we deal with conflict biblically, it can serve as a stimulus to learn and an opportunity for positive spiritual and relational growth.

The next thing we need to do is examine how Jesus addressed conflicts and emulate Him. He dealt with them head on and immediately. The Lord was very clear about conflict resolution in what He said in the Sermon on the Mount:

> *"Therefore if thou bring thy gift to the altar, and there rememberest that thy brother hath ought against thee;*
>
> *"Leave there thy gift before the altar, and go thy way; first be reconciled to thy brother, and then come and offer thy gift."*—Matthew 5:23, 24.

In saying this, the Lord is dealing with conflict as a sin and points out that a gift to Him from someone who is avoiding conflict resolution is unacceptable. The application for us is simple: we need to deal with conflict immediately in order to remain in fellowship with our Lord.

In most cases, going to a person with whom you have a conflict and talking it over with love will resolve it. I cannot tell you how many families and marriages I've witnessed the Lord heal in this way. If we submit to the Lord's plan, we will receive His blessings.

In a very few cases, there may be a conflict that we cannot resolve in the first conversation. Here's how the Lord says to deal with those individuals:

"Moreover if thy brother shall trespass against thee, go and tell him his fault between thee and him alone: if he shall hear thee, thou hast gained thy brother.

"But if he will not hear thee, then take with thee one or two more, that in the mouth of two or three witnesses every word may be established.

"And if he shall neglect to hear them, tell it unto the church: but if he neglect to hear the church, let him be unto thee as an heathen man and a publican."— Matthew 18:15–17.

Throughout these verses the Lord is addressing the sin of conflict. Every time I study these verses I am reminded that the Lord does not choose sides. He looks at conflict and hates it; He wants it resolved for the sake of fellowship with His people. But He understands that in some cases some folks will not be willing to listen.

My point is that neither PTSD nor any other problem is an excuse to live with unresolved conflict. Please don't misunderstand. God cares for His children, and He is grieved by your conflicts. However, He gives you a way out. Follow your orders and move out smartly. All you need to do is trust Him and implement His plan.

Let's review His plan. First, if there is a person you're having a conflict with, go to that person as soon as possible and address the issues face to face. Avoid involving anyone else.

Next, if you cannot resolve the disagreement, take a couple of folks from church with you to the person with whom you're having a conflict and try again to resolve the problem. If the offended person still does not respond, give the situation to the Lord. In the Lord's eyes you are free of the conflict.

Some may think this seems like an overly formal way to deal with a family member. That's not true! This is exactly how you should deal with anybody. It is the only approach that comes with the Lord's power.

If you desire to be set free from your tendency to have conflicts and if you desire to have Heaven as your final home, there are several steps you must follow.

First, you must understand that you are a sinner. The Bible states, "For all have sinned, and come short of the glory of God" (Romans 3:23). All people are sinners and do not deserve to go to Heaven.

Second, you must realize that your sin has deadly consequences. Romans 6:23 says, "For the wages of sin is death." Here "death" refers to an eternal separation from God in Hell.

Third, you need to recognize that your sin debt has been paid. The Bible states, "God commendeth his love toward us, in that, while we were yet sinners, Christ died for us" (Romans 5:8). Jesus Christ, the Son of God, took your punishment when He died for you!

Fourth, you must repent of your sins. "God...now commandeth all men every where to repent" (Acts 17:30). Repentance is a change of heart that causes you to turn toward God and away from your present way of life.

Finally, you must take action to ensure the Lord knows your intentions.

> *"If thou shalt confess with thy mouth the Lord Jesus, and shalt believe in thine heart that God hath raised him from the dead, thou shalt be saved.*
>
> *"For with the heart man believeth unto righteousness; and with the mouth confession is made unto salvation."*— Romans 10:9, 10.

This passage lists two aspects of salvation. You are required to confess that Jesus is Lord and also to believe in your heart that God resurrected Him. Until you do these two things, you are still on your way to Hell.

When you agreed to serve your country, community or family, you believed the promises made to you by the recruiter or partner, and you acted on those promises. To become a Christian, you must believe God's promises and act on them by asking Him to save you. God cannot lie! Here is His promise to you: "He that believeth on the Son hath everlasting life: and he that believeth not the Son shall not see life; but the wrath of God abideth on him" (John 3:36).

If you will accept Jesus Christ as your Saviour, please pray this prayer or one similar to it:

> Lord Jesus, I admit I am a sinner going to Hell. I know that I cannot save myself. I repent of my sins and put my faith in the blood that You shed for me on the cross to pay for all my sins. I now accept You as my Saviour and trust You to take me to Heaven. Thank You for saving me. Amen.

If you prayed for Christ to save you and meant it in your heart, you're saved. However, if you didn't say that prayer or did not mean it in your heart, I pray that as you go through this book or think about this over the next couple of days, the Lord will prompt you to make things right.

Personal and Group Follow-Up

Memory Verses

"Let us therefore follow after the things which make for peace, and things wherewith one may edify another."—Romans 14:19.

"Therefore if thou bring thy gift to the altar, and there rememberest that thy brother hath ought against thee;

"Leave there thy gift before the altar, and go thy way; first be reconciled to thy brother, and then come and offer thy gift."—Matthew 5:23, 24.

Discussion Points

1. How does PTSD affect a person's marriage?

____

____

2. Resolving conflicts rather than avoiding them allows you to have ____________________ with God.

3. Does the Lord choose sides in a conflict?

____

4. Name three things you learned from this lesson.

____

____

____

____

____

____

____

____

5. Would you like to share a testimony with the group about your study of this chapter?_______________

8 The Bible on Apathy

"The way of the slothful man is as an hedge of thorns: but the way of the righteous is made plain."—Proverbs 15:19.

Bible Preparation

"The soul of the sluggard desireth, and hath nothing: but the soul of the diligent shall be made fat."—Proverbs 13:4.

"And whatsoever ye do, do it heartily, as to the Lord, and not unto men."—Colossians 3:23.

"For even when we were with you, this we commanded you, that if any would not work, neither should he eat."—II Thessalonians 3:10.

"He becometh poor that dealeth with a slack hand: but the hand of the diligent maketh rich."—Proverbs 10:4.

"He also that is slothful in his work is brother to him that is a great waster."—Proverbs 18:9.

"But if any provide not for his own, and specially for those of his own house, he hath denied the faith, and is worse than an infidel."—I Timothy 5:8.

"The desire of the slothful killeth him; for his hands refuse to labour."—Proverbs 21:25.

"The sluggard will not plow by reason of the cold; therefore shall he beg in harvest, and have nothing."

"Love not sleep, lest thou come to poverty; open thine eyes, and thou shalt be satisfied with bread."—Proverbs 20:4, 13.

"Slothfulness casteth into a deep sleep; and an idle soul shall suffer hunger."—Proverbs 19:15.

"But Jesus answered them, My Father worketh hitherto, and I work."—John 5:17.

"Go to the ant, thou sluggard; consider her ways, and be wise."—Proverbs 6:6.

"The hand of the diligent shall bear rule: but the slothful shall be under tribute."—Proverbs 12:24.

"But to do good and to communicate forget not: for with such sacrifices God is well pleased."—Hebrews 13:16.

"But be ye doers of the word, and not hearers only, deceiving your own selves."—James 1:22.

"In all labour there is profit: but the talk of the lips tendeth only to penury."—Proverbs 14:23.

"Therefore to him that knoweth to do good, and doeth it not, to him it is sin."—James 4:17.

"Study to shew thyself approved unto God, a workman that needeth not to be ashamed, rightly dividing the word of truth."—II Timothy 2:15.

In the army we had a derogatory expression to describe apathetic soldiers. We called them ROAD soldiers. It is an acronym that stands for Retired On Active Duty. To any soldier with half a heart and a love for his country, those were fighting words. They evoked emotions that generally led to a fight.

The odd thing is, most of the same people who felt like killing someone for tagging them with those words when they served in their jobs are ROAD soldiers in other areas of their lives, including serving God and family.

People who would stay up all night to learn a new weapon or cram for exams have no idea how many books are in the Bible or do not even know their spouses' favorite colors. One man admitted he didn't even know his son's birthdate. If we hope to succeed in life, we need our heads in the game.

Many people with PTSD have the symptom of apathy. The *American Dictionary of the English Language of 1828* defines *apathy* in the following way:

> Want of feeling; an utter privation of passion, or insensibility to pain; applied either to the body or the mind.

According to our Lord, apathy is much more than that. The Bible teaches, "Be watchful, and strengthen the things which remain, that are ready to die: for I have not found thy works perfect before God" (Revelation 3:2). In this verse we're challenged to be continually on watch. It reminds me of having guard duty in the military and being responsible for those who sleep. It's an awesome responsibility. If we let our guard down, people might die and the enemy can succeed. In God's view, life is the same way.

Many may remember the way our parents fixated on our first walk alone to the bus stop. Our parents had spent our entire lives to that point preparing us for that day. Our heads were on a swivel, and we were very aware of everything around us. Living for God requires the same level of awareness.

One way to think about it is that apathy is a cancer that eats away at awareness. People in the bondage of apathy will never experience complete victory in their lives.

Apathy, otherwise known as laziness, slothfulness or indifference, is the opposite of God's design for our lives. Think about it! It's like saying any greatness in our lives is in the past. It's giving up, and that never is acceptable.

The Bible teaches in John 15 that Christ is the true vine and we are His branches. That relationship is essential for the branch to produce fruit. A branch without the vine is a dying branch. When there is no effort to help or have a positive impact on others, our lives become stagnant.

In a way, apathy is a fear of change because something requires us to grow beyond our comfort level. Resisting godly change in our lives is being stuck in a backsliding mode that births more symptoms like gossip, pride, hatred, and slander. Sadly, these hate-based symptoms take the place of healthy enthusiasm and drive.

Apathy is a serious sin and is an affront to our Lord. Let's look at Revelation 3:16 for a better understanding of the severity of this condition: "So then because thou art lukewarm, and neither cold nor hot, I will spue thee out of my mouth."

Lukewarm usually refers to water that has been sitting out at room temperature with no care. Often it can cause stomach problems such as vomiting.[38] People with apathy are compared to tainted water that makes people vomit.

As you can see, apathy is never acceptable to our Lord and stands in the way of great victories in our lives and in our families. But apathy is a problem that is easily conquered by the Lord.

If you desire to be free from apathy and to have Heaven as your final home, there are several steps you must follow.

First, you must understand that you are a sinner. The Bible states, "For all have sinned, and come short of the glory of God" (Romans 3:23). All people are sinners and do not deserve to go to Heaven.

Second, you must realize that your sin has deadly consequences. Romans 6:23 says, "For the wages of sin

---

[38] Albert Barnes, *Notes, Explanatory and Practical, on the Book of Revelation* (New York: Harper & Brothers Publishers, 1859), 124.

is death." Here "death" refers to an eternal separation from God in Hell.

Third, you need to recognize that your sin debt has been paid. The Bible states, "But God commendeth his love toward us, in that, while we were yet sinners, Christ died for us" (Romans 5:8). Jesus Christ, the Son of God, took your punishment when He died for you!

Fourth, you must repent of your sins. "God...now commandeth all men every where to repent" (Acts 17:30). Repentance is a change of heart that causes you to turn toward God and away from your present way of life.

Finally, you must take action to ensure the Lord knows your intentions.

> *"If thou shalt confess with thy mouth the Lord Jesus, and shalt believe in thine heart that God hath raised him from the dead, thou shalt be saved.*
>
> *"For with the heart man believeth unto righteousness; and with the mouth confession is made unto salvation."*— Romans 10:9, 10.

This passage lists two aspects of salvation. You are required to confess that Jesus is Lord and also to believe in your heart that God resurrected Him. Until you do these two things, you are still on your way to Hell.

When you agreed to serve your country, community or family, you believed the promises made to you by the recruiter or partner, and you acted on those promises. To become a Christian, you must believe God's promises and act on them by asking Him to save you. God cannot lie! Here is His promise to you: "He that believeth on the Son hath everlasting life: and he that believeth not the Son shall not see life; but the wrath of God abideth on him" (John 3:36).

If you will accept Jesus Christ as your Saviour, please pray this prayer or one similar to it:

> Lord Jesus, I admit I am a sinner going to Hell. I know that I cannot save myself. I repent of my sins and put my faith in the blood that You shed for me on the cross to pay for all my sins. I now accept You as my Saviour and trust You to take me to Heaven. Thank You for saving me. Amen.

If you prayed for Christ to save you and meant it in your heart, you're saved. However, if you didn't say that prayer or did not mean it in your heart, I pray that as you think about this over the next couple of days, the Lord will prompt you to make things right.

Personal and Group Follow-Up

Memory Verses

"The way of the slothful man is as an hedge of thorns: but the way of the righteous is made plain."—Proverbs 15:19.

"So then because thou art lukewarm, and neither cold nor hot, I will spue thee out of my mouth."—Revelation 3:16.

Discussion Points

1. In Revelation 3:2, we're challenged to be continually on ____.

2. One way to think about it is that apathy is a

____ that eats away at awareness.

3. Name three things you learned from this lesson.

____

____

____

____

4. Would you like to share a testimony with the group about what you learned from this chapter? ____

9 The Bible on Moral Injury

"There is therefore now no condemnation to them which are in Christ Jesus, who walk not after the flesh, but after the Spirit."—Romans 8:1.

Bible Preparation

"The LORD *redeemeth the soul of his servants: and none of them that trust in him shall be desolate."*—Psalm 34:22.

"The LORD *hath taken away thy judgments, he hath cast out thine enemy: the king of Israel, even the* LORD, *is in the midst of thee: thou shalt not see evil any more."*—Zephaniah 3:15.

Moral injury refers to an injury to an individual's moral conscience resulting from an act of perceived moral transgression which produces profound emotional shame.[39] The concept of moral injury emphasizes the psychological, cultural and spiritual aspects of trauma.

[39] Litz, B. T.; Stein, N.; Delaney, E.; Lebowitz, L.; Nash, W. P.; Silva, C.; Maguen, S. (11-12-2014). *Clin Psychol Rev. 29:* 695–706. doi:10.1016;j.cpr.2009.07.003. PMID 19683376.

Distinct from pathology, moral injury is a normal human response to an abnormal event.[40] The concept is currently used in literature about the mental health of military veterans who have witnessed or perpetrated an act in combat that transgressed their deeply held moral beliefs.[41]

Moral injury can also be experienced by those who have been transgressed against. For example, when one goes to war thinking that the purpose of the war is to eradicate weapons of mass destruction but finds that not to be the case, the warrior can experience moral injury.

Those who have seen and experienced death, mayhem, destruction, and violence have had their worldviews shattered—the sanctity of life, safety, love, health, peace, etc.—and can suffer moral injury as well.

What Is the Aftermath of Moral Injury?

In terms of the aftermath of moral injuries, acts of transgression may result in highly aversive and haunting states of inner conflict and turmoil. Emotional responses may include:

- Shame, which stems from global self-attributions (for example: "I am an evil, terrible person; I am unforgivable")
- Guilt
- Anxiety about possible consequences
- Anger about betrayal-based moral injuries

---

[40] Rita Nakashima and Gabriella Lettini, *Soul Repair: Recovering From Moral Injury After War* (Boston: Beacon Press, 2012).
[41] Shira Maguen, Brett Litz, "Moral Injury in the Context of War," PTSD: National Center for PTSD, U.S. Department of Veterans' Affairs. Retrieved December 13, 2015.

Behavioral manifestations of moral injury may include:

- Anomie (for example: alienation, purposelessness, and/or social instability caused by a breakdown in standards and values)
- Withdrawal and self-condemnation
- Self-harming (for example: suicidal ideation or attempts)
- Self-handicapping behaviors (for example, alcohol or drug use, self-sabotaging relationships, etc.)

Additionally, moral injury has been posited to result in the re-experiencing, emotional numbing, and avoidance symptoms of PTSD. In addition to grave suffering, these manifestations of moral injury may lead to under- or unemployment and failed or harmed relationships with loved ones and friends.

Can Killing Cause Moral Injury?

Several studies demonstrate an association between killing in war and mental and behavioral health problems, which may be proxies for moral injury. For example:

Across eras (Vietnam, Operations Desert Storm and Desert Shield, Operation Iraqi Freedom [OIF], Operation Enduring Freedom [OEF], etc.) **those who kill in war are at greater risk** for a number of mental health consequences and functional difficulties, including PTSD, after accounting for a number of demographic variables and other indicators of combat exposure.

In returning OIF veterans, even after controlling for combat exposure, **taking another life was a significant predictor** of PTSD symptoms, alcohol abuse, anger, and relationship problems.

Vietnam veterans who reported killing were twice as likely to report suicidal ideation as those who did not, even after accounting for general combat exposure, PTSD and depression diagnoses. In OIF veterans, the relationship between killing and suicidal ideation was mediated by PTSD and depression symptoms.

Killing in war may be an important indicator of risk for developing frequent and severe PTSD symptoms. Three-quarters of individuals who killed were in the two most severe PTSD symptom classes, and those who killed had twice the odds of being in the most symptomatic PTSD class, compared to those who did not kill. Those who endorsed killing a noncombatant or killing in the context of anger or revenge were more likely to belong to the most symptomatic PTSD class, compared to those who did not kill.

Although killing may be a precursor to moral injury, it is important to note that not all killing in war results in adverse outcomes for military personnel. As noted earlier, certain elements need to be present for moral injury to occur, including a perceived transgression that goes against individual or shared moral expectations.

For example, a military member who kills an enemy combatant in self-defense may perceive that the death was justified. If, however, a civilian was perceived to be armed and consequently killed, with military personnel later discovering that the individual was in fact unarmed, this may set the stage for the development of moral injury.

Are Moral Injury and PTSD the Same?

More research is needed to answer this question. At present, although the constructs of PTSD and moral injury overlap, each has unique components that make it a separable consequence of war and other traumatic contexts.

1. PTSD is a mental disorder that requires a diagnosis. Moral injury is a dimensional problem—there is no threshold for the presence of moral injury; rather, at a given point in time, a veteran may have none or mild to extreme manifestations.
2. Transgression is not necessary for PTSD to develop, nor does the PTSD diagnosis sufficiently capture moral injury (shame, self-handicapping, guilt, etc.).

Consequently, it is important to assess mental health symptoms and moral injury as separate manifestations of war trauma to form a comprehensive clinical picture and provide the most relevant treatment. One example of a moral injury specific measure is the Moral Injury Events Scale.

Biblical Just War

"Then said Jesus unto him, Put up again thy sword into his place: for all they that take the sword shall perish with the sword."—Matthew 26:52.

"A time to love, and a time to hate; a time of war, and a time of peace."—Ecclesiastes 3:8.

"Blessed are the peacemakers: for they shall be called the children of God."—Matthew 5:9.

"Think not that I am come to send peace on earth: I came not to send peace, but a sword."—Matthew 10:34.

"And ye shall hear of wars and rumours of wars: see that ye be not troubled: for all these things must come to pass, but the end is not yet.

"For nation shall rise against nation, and kingdom against kingdom: and there shall be famines, and pestilences, and earthquakes, in divers places."—Matthew 24:6, 7.

Why Is "Thou Shalt Not Kill" in the Ten Commandments?

Commandment Number Six (Exodus 20:13) forbids the unjustified taking of a human life. However, the commandment itself has a couple of interesting elements that bear mentioning.

First and foremost, different Bible translations give the appearance of different meanings, and there is potential for misunderstanding the actual meaning of the verse.

Second, man was never created for the act of murdering another, and there needs to be an explanation for such a violent and final act towards another human being.

Third, because of the translational challenge, we

need to understand the difference between "murder" and "killing."

And last but not least, how does God view murder? To God, murder is not just physical in nature but also the condition of one's heart towards another.

There are two different Hebrew words (*ratsakh, mut*) and two Greek words (*phoneuo, apokteino*) for "murder" and "killing." One means "to put to death," and the other means "to murder." The latter one is the one prohibited by the Ten Commandments, not the former. In fact, *ratsakh* has a broader definition than the English word *murder. Ratsakh* also covers deaths due to carelessness or neglect but is never used when describing killing during wartime.[42]

Personal and Group Follow-Up

Memory Verse

"A time to love, and a time to hate; a time of war, and a time of peace."—Ecclesiastes 3:8.

Discussion Points

1. What is the aftermath of moral injury?

____

____

____

____

2. Give examples of self-harming.______________

[42] GotQuestions.org. https://www.gotquestions.org/you-shall-not-murder.html.

3. Give examples of self-handicapping behaviors.

4. Questions I have or points I'd like to share with the group.

10 The Bible on Pornography

"I will set no wicked thing before mine eyes: I hate the work of them that turn aside; it shall not cleave to me."—Psalm 101:3.

According to Paul Fishbein, founder of Adult Video News, "Porn doesn't have a demographic—it goes across all demographics." After an analysis of 400 million web searches, researchers concluded that one in eight of all searches online are for erotic content.[43]

Who is more likely to seek out pornography online? According to data taken from Internet users who took part in the general social survey:

1. Men are 543 percent more likely to look at porn than females.

2. Those who are politically more liberal are 19 percent more likely to look at porn.

3. Those who have ever committed adultery are 218

---

[43] Paul Fishbein, *Women Trendsetting,* page 23, AVN.

percent more likely to look at porn.

4. Those who have ever engaged in paid sex are 270 percent more likely to look at porn.[44]

The Addiction

1. Those who are happily married are 61 percent less likely to look at porn.

2. Those with teen children at home are 45 percent less likely to look at porn.

3. Regular church attenders are 26 percent less likely to look at porn than non-attenders.

4. People with PTSD are twice as likely to suffer from a pornography addiction.

5. The American Academy of Matrimonial Lawyers reports that 56 percent of divorce cases involve one party's having "an obsessive interest in pornographic websites."

6. More than half of boys and nearly a third of girls see their first pornographic images before they turn thirteen. In a survey of hundreds of college students, 93 percent of boys and 62 percent of girls said they were exposed to pornography before they turned eighteen. In the same survey, 83 percent of boys and 57 percent of girls said they had seen images of group sex online.

7. "Online porn is to sex addiction what crack

[44] https://www.theatlantic.com/magazine/archive/2008/10/is-pornography-adultery/306989/, 10/13/17, "Is Pornography Adultery?" *The Atlantic,* April 2008.

cocaine is to drug addiction," says Robert Weiss, director of the Sexual Recovery Institute in Los Angeles. Weiss is a longtime sexual-addiction counselor who is helping the military set up treatment programs.[45]

Prolonged Exposure to Pornography Leads To

1. Married men or women who are involved in pornography feel less satisfied with their marriage relations and less emotionally attached to their spouses. Spouses notice and are upset by the difference.

2. Pornography use is a pathway to infidelity and divorce and is frequently a major factor in these family disasters.

3. Among couples affected by one spouse's addiction, two-thirds experience a loss of interest in sexual intercourse.

4. Both spouses perceive pornography viewing as tantamount to infidelity.

5. Pornography viewing leads to a loss of interest in good family relations.

6. Pornography is addictive, and neuroscientists are beginning to map the biological substrate of this addiction.

7. Users tend to become desensitized to the type of pornography they use, become bored with it, and then

---

[45] https://www.wol.org/2016/10/16/free-sexual-sin-pornography/Word of Life—10/15/16.

seek more perverse forms of pornography.

8. Men who view pornography regularly have a higher tolerance for abnormal sexuality, including rape, sexual aggression and sexual promiscuity.

9. Prolonged consumption of pornography by men produces stronger notions of women as commodities or as "sex objects."

10. Pornography engenders greater sexual permissiveness, which in turn leads to a greater risk of out-of-wedlock births and STDs. These, in turn, lead to still more weaknesses and debilities.

11. Child-sex offenders are more likely to view pornography regularly or to be involved in its distribution.

12. A complete disconnection to God and His plan for intimacy.[46]

Selected Bible Verses Against Pornography

> *"But I say unto you, That whosoever looketh on a woman to lust after her hath committed adultery with her already in his heart."*—Matthew 5:28.

The Lord is clear; if a man looks at women with lust (sexual desire) he is committing adultery. God views this as sin and we should not do it.

> *"I will set no wicked thing before mine eyes: I hate*

[46] "The Effects of Pornography on Individuals, Marriage, Family, and Community," Patrick F. Fagan, Ph.D., pages 3–6, *Family Guide to Movies*.

the work of them that turn aside; it shall not cleave to me."—Psalm 101:3.

By setting unclean things before our eyes we are subscribing to evil and it will become part of us. We should do whatever it takes to move away from evil.

"And the peace of God, which passeth all understanding, shall keep your hearts and minds through Christ Jesus.

"Finally, brethren, whatsoever things are true, whatsoever things are honest, whatsoever things are just, whatsoever things are pure, whatsoever things are lovely, whatsoever things are of good report; if there be any virtue, and if there be any praise, think on these things."—Philippians 4:7, 8.

The Lord admonishes us to keep pure and seek things which are pure.

"But if ye will not do so, behold, ye have sinned against the Lord*: and be sure your sin will find you out."*—Numbers 32:23.

We need to realize that the Lord sees us sin and nothing is hidden from His view.

"Take us the foxes, the little foxes, that spoil the vines: for our vines have tender grapes."—Song of Solomon 2:15.

In this verse, it explains that sometimes when foxes were in search of food they entered into the grape orchards devouring the grapes and spoiling the crop. However, little foxes were too small to reach the grape bunches so they would chew on the vines to bring down the grapes and it would kill the whole vine. Instead of the farmer just losing his crop, he would lose his vine, which was more disastrous, and that would force him to start all over. Spiritually, some things we do or allow that we might think are little or insignificant can also be disastrous for us.

The sin of pornography is one of the most devastating problems that have ensnared many good people. These same people will testify that they were ensnared with just a peek or a quick click on the Internet. Columbia University neurologist Doctor Norman Doidge, in his book *The Brain That Changes Itself,* describes how pornography causes rewiring of the neural circuits. He notes that in a study of men viewing Internet pornography, the men looked "uncannily" like rats pushing the levers in experimental Skinner boxes. "Like the addicted rats," Dr. Doidge points out, "the men were desperately seeking their next fix, clicking the mouse just as the rats pushed the lever."

This one little fox led to their downfall. Many, out of curiosity, just went to a site to see what was there. This is one of the Devil's tricks to get people ensnared. Satan is the power behind this attraction to forbidden sexual images. People that are trapped today can tell you there is an evil drawing that compels them to return again and again. Many desire to be free but seem hopelessly gripped by this evil desire. We want to share the good news—there is a way out through Jesus Christ.

In America and in many other nations of the world, our societies have become the most sexually saturated societies in human history. Sodom and Gomorrah might be the only exceptions. America's pornography industry is not only pervasive but powerful as well. It generates more than $14 billion in revenue annually. In America we have 4.2 million pornographic websites representing 12 percent of all websites. Unfortunately, this involvement is not limited to the non-Christian world; surveys reveal the Christian community is highly involved in this evil snare of perversion too. How did this happen? What can be done to help people get free from this bondage? What does the Bible offer as hope to those ensnared in sin?

As stated above, the research indicates that pornography can be extremely addictive. Ultimately, pornography conditions a person to respond emotionally and sexually to a self-centered, artificial world. Many online relationships are similar to pornography in that they are not based in reality; what individuals read and see about people, relationships and sex is distorted.

Viewing pornography can distort realistic views of healthy sexuality; lead to the objectification of women, men and/or children; and promote sexual gratification as a top emotional priority. Physical relationships are a gift from the Lord and are intended for marriage. The Devil uses pornography to distort that view and to keep people in bondage.

Every person finds ways to deal with the stress, anxiety, fear, boredom, and insecurity in his life. An addict is a person who has used addictive activities or substances as a way to deal with these things.

Because pornography is readily accessible and can serve as a way to cope with anxiety, fear, boredom, etc., it often is used.

Gene McConnell in an article called "The Stages of Pornography Addiction" from Focus on the Family lists the five stages of addiction to pornography as:

Early exposure. Most guys who get addicted to porn start early. They see the stuff when they are very young, and it gets its foot in the door.

Addiction. Later comes addiction. You keep coming back to porn. It becomes a regular part of your life. You're hooked. You can't quit.

Escalation. After a while, escalation begins. You start to look for more and more graphic porn. You start using porn that would have disgusted you when you started. Now it excites you.

Desensitization. Eventually, you start to become numb. Even the most graphic, degrading porn doesn't excite you anymore. You become desperate to feel the same thrill again but can't find it.

Acting out sexually. At this point, many men make a dangerous jump and start acting out sexually. They move from the paper and plastic images of porn to the real world.

How to Free Yourself From the Bondage of Pornography

1. You need first of all to repent of your sin and ask

Jesus to come into your heart and cleanse you and deliver you from this evil. No sin is too black or wicked that the blood of Jesus cannot cleanse you from it. The Bible says in I John 1:9–2:2,

> *"If we confess our sins, he is faithful and just to forgive us our sins, and to cleanse us from all unrighteousness.*
>
> *"If we say that we have not sinned, we make him a liar, and his word is not in us.*
>
> *"My little children, these things write I unto you, that ye sin not. And if any man sin, we have an advocate with the Father, Jesus Christ the righteous:*
>
> *"And he is the propitiation* [the atoning sacrifice] *for our sins: and not for ours only, but also for the sins of the whole world."*

2. Because pornography is a spiritual problem, you will need spiritual help in getting free from it. By partaking of this evil you have opened yourself up to demonic control. You may need someone who has the gift of the Holy Spirit to pray deliverance over you.

You should seek out a Bible-believing church that believes in deliverance and knows how to deal with demons. The Lord will lead you in this matter if you ask Him. Do not allow pride to prevent you from getting the needed help for getting free.

> *"Submit yourselves therefore to God. Resist the devil, and he will flee from you.*
>
> *"Draw nigh to God, and he will draw nigh to you. Cleanse your hands, ye sinners; and purify your hearts, ye double minded."*—James 4:7, 8.

3. As you commit your life to Christ and obey Him, you can get the victory because you are not fighting this battle alone but you have access to the power of Christ and what He did for you.

> *"Let not sin therefore reign in your mortal body, that ye should obey it in the lusts thereof.*
>
> *"Neither yield ye your members as instruments of unrighteousness unto sin: but yield yourselves unto God, as those that are alive from the dead, and your members as instruments of righteousness unto God.*
>
> *"For sin shall not have dominion over you: for ye are not under the law, but under grace.*
>
> *"What then? shall we sin, because we are not under the law, but under grace? God forbid.*
>
> *"Know ye not, that to whom ye yield yourselves servants to obey, his servants ye are to whom ye obey; whether of sin unto death, or of obedience unto righteousness?*
>
> *"But God be thanked, that ye were the servants of sin, but ye have obeyed from the heart that form of doctrine which was delivered you.*
>
> *"Being then made free from sin, ye became the servants of righteousness."*—Romans 6:12–18.

4. Today men and women must war in this culture to maintain their sexual purity. This battle is a battle in the mind. You must cast down imaginations that do not agree with the Bible and quote the Word of God over your body and mind.

> *"For though we walk in the flesh, we do not war after the flesh:*
>
> *"(For the weapons of our warfare are not carnal, but*

mighty through God to the pulling down of strong holds;)

"Casting down imaginations, and every high thing that exalteth itself against the knowledge of God, and bringing into captivity every thought to the obedience of Christ."—II Corinthians 10:3–5.

5. You must stay away from the area of temptation and destroy all videos, games, magazines, etc., that are pornographic. If you must use the computer in your work environment, you should employ a filter service for your ISP or software that filters out those evil invitations so they do not enter your e-mail and cannot be accessed by your browser.

"Flee fornication. Every sin that a man doeth is without the body; but he that committeth fornication sinneth against his own body.

"What? know ye not that your body is the temple of the Holy Ghost which is in you, which ye have of God, and ye are not your own?

"For ye are bought with a price: therefore glorify God in your body, and in your spirit, which are God's."—I Corinthians 6:18–20.

6. Should you stumble or fall, do not stay down. Just ask the Lord to forgive you and start again in your walk with Him. Ask Him to empower you to overcome. You cannot do it in your strength. Just remember that in Him you can do all things.

"I can do all things through Christ which strengtheneth me."—Philippians 4:13.

7. You need to yoke up with a Bible-believing

church. You can contact us at afbmissions.com and we'll be glad to recommend a local church.

Recommended Checks

If you know someone who has struggled to maintain purity in this area, may I recommend several checks to help him or her? Consider the following.

1. Modem filters.

2. Enroll the family in Covenant Eyes. Covenant Eyes is online software that monitors websites visited.

3. Allow each partner to check the computers for search history.

4. Pastoral or Christian counseling beginning weekly and slowly tapering off.

5. Using an activity journal which measures success and failures.

6. For spouses where infidelity has occurred, I recommend medical testing for the spouse who was unfaithful and if relations continued with the other spouse, I recommend both be tested.

Summary

In summary, many were ensnared by just a quick peek, a click or just a little curiosity in regard to pornography. Don't allow any little things that could lead to a pornography addiction. Racy movies, TV shows, books, calendars or pictures of naked women, X-rated magazines or movies with erotic sexual scenes are just a few of the things that can open the door for a greater entanglement in the pornography trap.

Remember, the Lord admonishes us to keep pure and seek things which are pure. Stay clear of those things that will hook you into this addictive pattern.

Perhaps some of you reading this book may have already developed an addiction to porn. If you see in your life any of the patterns described here, you need to put on the brakes right now. So the questions are: "Is porn beginning to control your life? Does it seem you cannot put it down? Do you keep going back for more?"

Maybe you find yourself needing to see increasingly more graphic pornography. You're starting to take risks or act out physically for sexual thrills.

If you see yourself at any point on this progression, you are in serious trouble and you need to realize it. Please contact your doctor and contact us at afbmissions.com to help you find a church where you can receive counseling.

Appendix

Put Off Sinful Behavior; Put On Godly Behavior

"That ye put off concerning the former conversation the old man, which is corrupt according to the deceitful lusts;

"And be renewed in the spirit of your mind;

"And that ye put on the new man, which after God is created in righteousness and true holiness.

"Wherefore putting away lying, speak every man truth with his neighbour: for we are members one of another.

"Be ye angry, and sin not: let not the sun go down upon your wrath:

"Neither give place to the devil.

"Let him that stole steal no more: but rather let him labour, working with his hands the thing which is good, that he may have to give to him that needeth.

"Let no corrupt communication proceed out of your mouth, but that which is good to the use of edifying, that it may minister grace unto the hearers.

"And grieve not the holy Spirit of God, whereby ye are sealed unto the day of redemption.

"Let all bitterness, and wrath, and anger, and clamour, and evil speaking, be put away from you, with all malice:

"And be ye kind one to another, tenderhearted, forgiving one another, even as God for Christ's sake hath forgiven you."—Ephesians 4:22–32.

Put off adultery. Put on fidelity.

"Ye have heard that it was said by them of old time, Thou shalt not commit adultery:

"But I say unto you, That whosoever looketh on a woman to lust after her hath committed adultery with her already in his heart."—Matthew 5:27, 28.

"Thou shalt not commit adultery."—Exodus 20:14.

Put off anger, losing your temper and/or wrath. Put on self-control.

"Wherefore, my beloved brethren, let every man be swift to hear, slow to speak, slow to wrath."—James 1:19.

"He that is soon angry dealeth foolishly: and a man of wicked devices is hated."—Proverbs 14:17.

"He that is slow to anger is better than the mighty; and he that ruleth his spirit than he that taketh a city."—Proverbs 16:32.

"And not only so, but we glory in tribulations also: knowing that tribulation worketh patience;

"And patience, experience; and experience, hope."—Romans 5:3, 4.

"And they that are Christ's have crucified the flesh with the affections and lusts.

"If we live in the Spirit, let us also walk in the Spirit."—Galatians 5:24, 25.

Put off bad language/profanity. Put on language that edifies.

"As he loved cursing, so let it come unto him: as he delighted not in blessing, so let it be far from him."—Psalm 109:17.

"Let no corrupt communication proceed out of your mouth, but that which is good to the use of edifying, that it may minister grace unto the hearers."—Ephesians 4:29.

"Let no man despise thy youth; but be thou an example of the believers, in word, in conversation, in charity, in spirit, in faith, in purity."—I Timothy 4:12.

Put off bad motives. Put on meditation on God.

"But the LORD *said unto Samuel, Look not on his countenance, or on the height of his stature; because I have refused him: for the* LORD *seeth not as man seeth; for man looketh on the outward appearance, but the* LORD *looketh on the heart."*—I Samuel 16:7.

"Let the words of my mouth, and the meditation of my heart, be acceptable in thy sight, O LORD, *my strength, and my redeemer."*—Psalm 19:14.

Put off being inhospitable. Put on being hospitable.

"Use hospitality one to another without grudging."—I Peter 4:9.

"Distributing to the necessity of saints; given to hospitality."—Romans 12:13.

Put off being a part of the worldly crowd. Put on being a part of the body of Christ.

"For what shall it profit a man, if he shall gain the whole world, and lose his own soul?"—Mark 8:36.

"But seek ye first the kingdom of God, and his righteousness; and all these things shall be added unto you."—Matthew 6:33.

Put off being a stumbling block. Put on being a steppingstone.

"But take heed lest by any means this liberty of yours become a stumblingblock to them that are weak.

"For if any man see thee which hast knowledge sit at meat in the idol's temple, shall not the conscience of him which is weak be emboldened to eat those things which are offered to idols;

"And through thy knowledge shall the weak brother perish, for whom Christ died?"—I Corinthians 8:9–11.

"It is good neither to eat flesh, nor to drink wine, nor any thing whereby thy brother stumbleth, or is offended, or is made weak."—Romans 14:21.

Put off bitterness. Put on tenderheartedness.

"Looking diligently lest any man fail of the grace of God; lest any root of bitterness springing up trouble you, and thereby many be defiled."—Hebrews 12:15.

"Put on therefore, as the elect of God, holy and beloved, bowels of mercies, kindness, humbleness of mind, meekness, longsuffering."—Colossians 3:12.

Put off boasting. Put on humility.

"For who maketh thee to differ from another? and what hast thou that thou didst not receive? now if thou didst receive it, why dost thou glory, as if thou hadst not received it?"—I Corinthians 4:7.

"Let another man praise thee, and not thine own mouth; a stranger, and not thine own lips."—Proverbs 27:2.

Put off bodily harm. Put on gentleness.

"A violent man enticeth his neighbour, and leadeth him into the way that is not good."—Proverbs 16:29.

"But we were gentle among you, even as a nurse cherisheth her children."—I Thessalonians 2:7.

Put off cheating. Put on honesty.

"The eyes of the LORD are in every place, beholding the evil and the good."—Proverbs 15:3.

"But that on the good ground are they, which in an honest and good heart, having heard the word, keep it, and bring forth fruit with patience."—Luke 8:15.

Put off complacency. Put on diligence.

"Therefore to him that knoweth to do good, and doeth it not, to him it is sin."—James 4:17.

"And whatsoever ye do, do it heartily, as to the Lord, and not unto men."—Colossians 3:23.

Put off complaining. Put on contentment.

"To execute judgment upon all, and to convince all that are ungodly among them of all their ungodly deeds which they have ungodly committed, and of all their hard

speeches which ungodly sinners have spoken against him.

"These are murmurers, complainers, walking after their own lusts; and their mouth speaketh great swelling words, having men's persons in admiration because of advantage."—Jude 15, 16.

Put off "copping out." Put on discipline.

"Wherefore if they shall say unto you, Behold, he is in the desert; go not forth: behold, he is in the secret chambers; believe it not."—Matthew 24:26.

"And whosoever doth not bear his cross, and come after me, cannot be my disciple."—Luke 14:27.

Put off covetousness. Put on yielding of rights.

"Thou shalt not covet thy neighbour's house, thou shalt not covet thy neighbour's wife, nor his manservant, nor his maidservant, nor his ox, nor his ass, nor any thing that is thy neighbour's."—Exodus 20:17.

"Mortify therefore your members which are upon the earth; fornication, uncleanness, inordinate affection, evil concupiscence, and covetousness, which is idolatry."—Colossians 3:5.

"Let your conversation be without covetousness; and be content with such things as ye have: for he hath said, I will never leave thee, nor forsake thee."—Hebrews 13:5.

Put off dancing. Put on glorifying God.

"Abstain from all appearance of evil."—I Thessalonians 5:22.

"Whether therefore ye eat, or drink, or whatsoever ye do, do all to the glory of God."—I Corinthians 10:31.

Put off dating the wrong person. Put on being equally yoked.

"Be ye not unequally yoked together with unbelievers: for what fellowship hath righteousness with unrighteousness? and what communion hath light with darkness?"—II Corinthians 6:14.

"All things are lawful unto me, but all things are not expedient: all things are lawful for me, but I will not be brought under the power of any."—I Corinthians 6:12.

Put off discontentment. Put on satisfaction.

"Not that I speak in respect of want: for I have learned, in whatsoever state I am, therewith to be content.

"I know both how to be abased, and I know how to abound: every where and in all things I am instructed both to be full and to be hungry, both to abound and to suffer need.

"I can do all things through Christ which strengtheneth me."—Philippians 4:11–13.

"Let your conversation be without covetousness; and be content with such things as ye have: for he hath said, I will never leave thee, nor forsake thee."—Hebrews 13:5.

Put off disobedience. Put on obedience.

"But if ye will not obey the voice of the LORD, but rebel against the commandment of the LORD, then shall the hand of the LORD be against you, as it was against your fathers."—I Samuel 12:15.

"And being made perfect, he became the author of eternal salvation unto all them that obey him."—Hebrews 5:9.

Put off doing less than your best. Put on doing your best.

"Whatsoever thy hand findeth to do, do it with thy might; for there is no work, nor device, nor knowledge, nor wisdom, in the grave, whither thou goest."—Ecclesiastes 9:10.

"And whatsoever ye do, do it heartily, as to the Lord, and not unto men."—Colossians 3:23.

Put off doubt and unbelief. Put on faith.

"Faithful is he that calleth you, who also will do it."—I Thessalonians 5:24.

"Now faith is the substance of things hoped for, the evidence of things not seen."—Hebrews 11:1.

Put off drinking. Put on being God's temple.

"Be not among winebibbers; among riotous eaters of flesh."

"Who hath woe? who hath sorrow? who hath contentions? who hath babbling? who hath wounds without cause? who hath redness of eyes?

"They that tarry long at the wine; they that go to seek mixed wine.

"Look not thou upon the wine when it is red, when it giveth his colour in the cup, when it moveth itself aright.

"At the last it biteth like a serpent, and stingeth like an adder.

"Thine eyes shall behold strange women, and thine heart shall utter perverse things."—Proverbs 23:20, 29–33.

Put off drugs and/or smoking. Put on being God's temple.

"But the fearful, and unbelieving, and the abominable, and murderers, and whoremongers, and sorcerers, and idolaters, and all liars, shall have their part in the lake which burneth with fire and brimstone: which is the second death."—Revelation 21:8.

"Know ye not that ye are the temple of God, and that the Spirit of God dwelleth in you?

"In any man defile the temple of God, him shall God destroy; for the temple of God is holy, which temple ye are.

"Let no man deceive himself. If any man among you seemeth to be wise in this world, let him become a fool, that he may be wise.

"For the wisdom of this world is foolishness with God. For it is written, He taketh the wise in their own craftiness.

"And again, The Lord knoweth the thoughts of the wise, that they are vain."—I Corinthians 3:16–20.

Put off evil thoughts. Put on right thinking.

"For as he thinketh in his heart, so is he: Eat and drink, saith he to thee; but his heart is not with thee."—Proverbs 23:7.

"Finally, brethren, whatsoever things are true, whatsoever things are honest, whatsoever things are just, whatsoever things are pure, whatsoever things are lovely, whatsoever things are of good report; if there be any virtue, and if there be any praise, think on these things."—Philippians 4:8.

Put off fornication. Put on purity.

"For this is the will of God, even your sanctification, that ye should abstain from fornication:

"That every one of you should know how to possess his vessel in sanctification and honour;

"Not in the lust of concupiscence, even as the Gentiles which know not God:

"That no man go beyond and defraud his brother in any matter: because that the Lord is the avenger of all such, as we also have forewarned you and testified.

"For God hath not called us unto uncleanness, but unto holiness."—I Thessalonians 4:3–7.

Put off gossip. Put on speaking with praise.

"And withal they learn to be idle, wandering about from house to house; and not only idle, but tattlers also and busybodies, speaking things which they ought not."—I Timothy 5:13.

"Let us therefore follow after the things which make for peace, and things wherewith one may edify another."—Romans 14:19.

Put off hatred. Put on love and kindness.

"Ye have heard that it was said by them of old time, Thou shalt not kill; and whosoever shall kill shall be in danger of the judgment:

"But I say unto you, That whosoever is angry with his brother without a cause shall be in danger of the judgment: and whosoever shall say to his brother, Raca, shall be in danger of the council: but whosoever shall say, Thou fool, shall be in danger of hell fire."—Matthew 5:21, 22.

"And though I bestow all my goods to feed the poor, and though I give my body to be burned, and have not charity, it profiteth me nothing."—I Corinthians 13:3.

Put off homosexuality. Put on God's purpose.

"For this cause God gave them up unto vile affections: for even their women did change the natural use into that which is against nature:

"And likewise also the men, leaving the natural use of the woman, burned in their lust one toward another; men with men working that which is unseemly, and receiving in themselves that recompence of their error which was meet."—Romans 1:26, 27.

"Lay hands suddenly on no man, neither be partaker of other men's sins: keep thyself pure."—I Timothy 5:22.

Put off hypocrisy. Put on honesty.

"So are the paths of all that forget God; and the hypocrite's hope shall perish."—Job 8:13.

"Wherefore putting away lying, speak every man truth with his neighbour: for we are members one of another."—Ephesians 4:25.

Put off idle words. Put on a bridled tongue.

"But I say unto you, That every idle word that men shall speak, they shall give account thereof in the day of judgment."—Matthew 12:36.

"Whoso keepeth his mouth and his tongue keepeth his soul from troubles."—Proverbs 21:23.

Put off idolatry. Put on giving Jesus Christ preeminence.

"Take heed to yourselves, that your heart be not deceived, and ye turn aside, and serve other gods, and worship them."—Deuteronomy 11:16.

"One God and Father of all, who is above all, and through all, and in you all."—Ephesians 4:6.

Put off immodesty. Put on modesty.

"As a jewel of gold in a swine's snout, so is a fair woman which is without discretion."—Proverbs 11:22.

"For the love of Christ constraineth us; because we thus judge, that if one died for all, then were all dead."—II Corinthians 5:14.

Put off impatience. Put on patience.

"My brethren, count it all joy when ye fall into divers temptations;

"Knowing this, that the trying of your faith worketh patience.

"But let patience have her perfect work, that ye may be perfect and entire, wanting nothing."—James 1:2–4.

"In your patience possess ye your souls."—Luke 21:19.

Put off improper relationships. Put on God's standard.

"Be not deceived: evil communications corrupt good manners."—I Corinthians 15:33.

"According to my earnest expectation and my hope, that in nothing I shall be ashamed, but that with all

boldness, as always, so now also Christ shall be magnified in my body, whether it be by life, or by death."—Philippians 1:20.

Put off irritation with others. Put on preference with love.

"Go not forth hastily to strive, lest thou know not what to do in the end thereof, when thy neighbour hath put thee to shame."—Proverbs 25:8.

"Let nothing be done through strife or vainglory; but in lowliness of mind let each esteem other better than themselves.

"Look not every man on his own things, but every man also on the things of others."—Philippians 2:3, 4.

Put off jealousy. Put on love.

"Wrath is cruel, and anger is outrageous; but who is able to stand before envy?"—Proverbs 27:4.

"Charity suffereth long, and is kind; charity envieth not; charity vaunteth not itself, is not puffed up."—I Corinthians 13:4.

Put off judging others. Put on searching of own sins.

"Judge not, that ye be not judged.

"For with what judgment ye judge, ye shall be judged: and with what measure ye mete, it shall be measured to you again."—Matthew 7:1, 2.

"And they which heard it, being convicted by their own conscience, went out one by one, beginning at the eldest, even unto the last: and Jesus was left alone, and

the woman standing in the midst."—John 8:9.

Put off lack of concern for lost souls. Put on winning souls to Christ.

"The fruit of the righteous is a tree of life; and he that winneth souls is wise."—Proverbs 11:30.

Put off lack of love. Put on the love of God.

"Beloved, let us love one another: for love is of God; and every one that loveth is born of God, and knoweth God.

"He that loveth not knoweth not God; for God is love."

"If a man say, I love God, and hateth his brother, he is a liar: for he that loveth not his brother whom he hath seen, how can he love God whom he hath not seen?"—I John 4:7, 8, 20.

"This is my commandment, That ye love one another, as I have loved you."—John 15:12.

Put off lack of moderation. Put on a balanced life.

"Let your moderation be known unto all men. The Lord is at hand."—Philippians 4:5.

Put off lack of rejoicing always. Put on rejoicing.

"Rejoice in the Lord alway: and again I say, Rejoice."—Philippians 4:4.

"Rejoice evermore."—I Thessalonians 5:16.

Put off lack of submission and/or disrespect. Put on a broken will.

"For of this sort are they which creep into houses, and

lead captive silly women laden with sins, led away with divers lusts."—II Timothy 3:6.

"Thy kingdom come. Thy will be done in earth, as it is in heaven."—Matthew 6:10.

Put off laziness. Put on diligence.

"See then that ye walk circumspectly, not as fools, but as wise,

"Redeeming the time, because the days are evil."—Ephesians 5:15, 16.

"Go to the ant, thou sluggard; consider her ways, and be wise:

"Which having no guide, overseer, or ruler,

"Provideth her meat in the summer, and gathereth her food in the harvest.

"How long wilt thou sleep, O sluggard? when wilt thou arise out of thy sleep?

"Yet a little sleep, a little slumber, a little folding of the hands to sleep:

"So shall thy poverty come as one that travelleth, and thy want as an armed man."—Proverbs 6:6–11.

Put off loss of first love. Put on meditating on Christ.

"Nevertheless I have somewhat against thee, because thou hast left thy first love."—Revelation 2:4.

"Herein is love, not that we loved God, but that he loved us, and sent his Son to be the propitiation for our sins."

"We love him, because he first loved us."—I John 4:10, 19.

Put off lust of the eyes. Put on pure thoughts.

"For all that is in the world, the lust of the flesh, and the lust of the eyes, and the pride of life, is not of the Father, but is of the world."—I John 2:16.

"Look not every man on his own things, but every man also on the things of others."—Philippians 2:4.

Put off the lust of the flesh. Put on pure desires.

"For all that is in the world, the lust of the flesh, and the lust of the eyes, and the pride of life, is not of the Father, but is of the world."—I John 2:16.

"Dearly beloved, I beseech you as strangers and pilgrims, abstain from fleshly lusts, which war against the soul."—I Peter 2:11.

Put off lying. Put on speaking the truth.

"Wherefore putting away lying, speak every man truth with his neighbour: for we are members one of another."—Ephesians 4:25.

"These are the things that ye shall do; Speak ye every man the truth to his neighbour; execute the judgment of truth and peace in your gates."—Zechariah 8:16.

Put off movies. Put on being a godly example.

"For as he thinketh in his heart, so is he: Eat and drink, saith he to thee; but his heart is not with thee."—Proverbs 23:7.

"Ye are our epistle written in our hearts, known and read of all men."—II Corinthians 3:2.

Put off murder. Put on love and kindness.

"Thou shalt not kill."—Exodus 20:13.

"Love worketh no ill to his neighbour: therefore love is the fulfilling of the law."—Romans 13:10.

Put off murmuring. Put on gratefulness.

"The foolishness of man perverteth his way: and his heart fretteth against the Lord."—Proverbs 19:3.

"Neither murmur ye, as some of them also murmured, and were destroyed of the destroyer."—I Corinthians 10:10.

Put off necking and/or petting. Put on abstinence.

"Now concerning the things whereof ye wrote unto me: It is good for a man not to touch a woman."—I Corinthians 7:1.

"That every one of you should know how to possess his vessel in sanctification and honour."—I Thessalonians 4:4.

Put off neglect of Bible study. Put on daily devotions.

"But continue thou in the things which thou hast learned and hast been assured of, knowing of whom thou hast learned them;

"And that from a child thou hast known the holy scriptures, which are able to make thee wise unto salvation through faith which is in Christ Jesus.

"All scripture is given by inspiration of God, and is profitable for doctrine, for reproof, for correction, for instruction in righteousness:

"That the man of God may be perfect, throughly furnished unto all good works."—II Timothy 3:14–17.

"Wherewithal shall a young man cleanse his way? by taking heed thereto according to thy word.

"With my whole heart have I sought thee: O let me not wander from thy commandments.

"Thy word have I hid in mine heart, that I might not sin against thee."—Psalm 119:9–11.

Put off not tithing. Put on tithing.

"Bring ye all the tithes into the storehouse, that there may be meat in mine house, and prove me now herewith, saith the LORD of hosts, if I will not open you the windows of heaven, and pour you out a blessing, that there shall not be room enough to receive it."—Malachi 3:10.

"But this I say, He which soweth sparingly shall reap also sparingly; and he which soweth bountifully shall reap also bountifully.

"Every man according as he purposeth in his heart, so let him give; not grudgingly, or of necessity: for God loveth a cheerful giver."—II Corinthians 9:6, 7.

Put off not using talents. Put on perfecting abilities.

"But he that knew not, and did commit things worthy of stripes, shall be beaten with few stripes. For unto whomsoever much is given, of him shall be much required: and to whom men have committed much, of him they will ask the more."—Luke 12:48.

Put off overeating. Put on self-control.

"But I keep under my body, and bring it into subjection:

lest that by any means, when I have preached to others, I myself should be a castaway."—I Corinthians 9:27.

Put off poor conduct in church. Put on reverence.

"Not forsaking the assembling of ourselves together, as the manner of some is; but exhorting one another: and so much the more, as ye see the day approaching."—Hebrews 10:25.

"Keep thy foot when thou goest to the house of God, and be more ready to hear, than to give the sacrifice of fools: for they consider not that they do evil."—Ecclesiastes 5:1.

Put off prayerlessness. Put on praying.

"Pray without ceasing."—I Thessalonians 5:17.

"Evening, and morning, and at noon, will I pray, and cry aloud: and he shall hear my voice."—Psalm 55:17.

Put off preferential treatment. Put on fairness.

"My brethren, have not the faith of our Lord Jesus Christ, the Lord of glory, with respect of persons.

"For if there come unto your assembly a man with a gold ring, in goodly apparel, and there come in also a poor man in vile raiment;

"And ye have respect to him that weareth the gay clothing, and say unto him, Sit thou here in a good place; and say to the poor, Stand thou there; or sit here under my footstool:

"Are ye not then partial in yourselves, and are become judges of evil thoughts?

"Hearken, my beloved brethren, Hath not God chosen

the poor of this world rich in faith, and heirs of the kingdom which he hath promised to them that love him?

"But ye have despised the poor. Do not rich men oppress you, and draw you before the judgment seats?"—James 2:1–6.

"And as ye would that men should do to you, do ye also to them likewise."—Luke 6:31.

Put off presuming on the future. Put on patience.

"Go to now, ye that say, To day or to morrow we will go into such a city, and continue there a year, and buy and sell, and get gain:

"Whereas ye know not what shall be on the morrow. For what is your life? It is even a vapour, that appeareth for a little time, and then vanisheth away."—James 4:13, 14.

"Boast not thyself of to morrow; for thou knowest not what a day may bring forth."—Proverbs 27:1.

Put off pride. Put on humility.

"Pride goeth before destruction, and an haughty spirit before a fall."—Proverbs 16:18.

"But he giveth more grace. Wherefore he saith, God resisteth the proud, but giveth grace unto the humble."—James 4:6.

Put off procrastination. Put on discipline.

"Boast not thyself of to morrow; for thou knowest not what a day may bring forth."—Proverbs 27:1.

"Consider the ravens: for they neither sow nor reap; which neither have storehouse nor barn; and God feedeth

them: how much more are ye better than the fowls?

"And which of you with taking thought can add to his stature one cubit?

"If ye then be not able to do that thing which is least, why take ye thought for the rest?

"Consider the lilies how they grow: they toil not, they spin not; and yet I say unto you, that Solomon in all his glory was not arrayed like one of these.

"If then God so clothe the grass, which is to day in the field, and to morrow is cast into the oven; how much more will he clothe you, O ye of little faith?

"And seek not ye what ye shall eat, or what ye shall drink, neither be ye of doubtful mind.

"For all these things do the nations of the world seek after: and your Father knoweth that ye have need of these things.

"But rather seek ye the kingdom of God; and all these things shall be added unto you."—Luke 12:24–31.

Put off rebellion. Put on submission to the Lord Jesus.

"For rebellion is as the sin of witchcraft, and stubbornness is as iniquity and idolatry. Because thou hast rejected the word of the LORD, he hath also rejected thee from being king."—I Samuel 15:23.

"Therefore also now, saith the LORD, turn ye even to me with all your heart, and with fasting, and with weeping, and with mourning:

"And rend your heart, and not your garments, and turn unto the LORD your God: for he is gracious and merciful, slow to anger, and of great kindness, and repenteth him of the evil."—Joel 2:12, 13.

Put off rock music. Put on music that edifies.

"For as he thinketh in his heart, so is he: Eat and drink, saith he to thee; but his heart is not with thee."—Proverbs 23:7.

"Speaking to yourselves in psalms and hymns and spiritual songs, singing and making melody in your heart to the Lord."—Ephesians 5:19.

Put off sassing. Put on respect for authority.

"Jesus therefore answered and said unto them, Murmur not among yourselves."—John 6:43.

"Speaking to yourselves in psalms and hymns and spiritual songs, singing and making melody in your heart to the Lord."—Ephesians 5:19.

Put off selfishness. Put on death to self.

"For all seek their own, not the things which are Jesus Christ's."—Philippians 2:21.

"Verily, verily, I say unto you, Except a corn of wheat fall into the ground and die, it abideth alone: but if it die, it bringeth forth much fruit."—John 12:24.

Put off speeding. Put on obedience.

"Submit yourselves to every ordinance of man for the Lord's sake: whether it be to the king, as supreme;

"Or unto governors, as unto them that are sent by him for the punishment of evildoers, and for the praise of them that do well."—I Peter 2:13, 14.

Put off stealing. Put on giving.

"Let him that stole steal no more: but rather let him labour, working with his hands the thing which is good,

that he may have to give to him that needeth."—Ephesians 4:28.

"Give, and it shall be given unto you; good measure, pressed down, and shaken together, and running over, shall men give into your bosom. For with the same measure that ye mete withal it shall be measured to you again."—Luke 6:38.

Put off strife. Put on esteeming others better than yourself.

"For where envying and strife is, there is confusion and every evil work."—James 3:16.

"But in lowliness of mind let each esteem other better than themselves."—Philippians 2:3.

"And as ye would that men should do to you, do ye also to them likewise."—Luke 6:31.

Put off stubbornness. Put on submission.

"For rebellion is as the sin of witchcraft, and stubbornness is as iniquity and idolatry. Because thou hast rejected the word of the Lord, *he hath also rejected thee from being king."*—I Samuel 15:23.

"Neither yield ye your members as instruments of unrighteousness unto sin: but yield yourselves unto God, as those that are alive from the dead, and your members as instruments of righteousness unto God."—Romans 6:13.

Put off temporary values. Put on eternal values.

"Lay not up for yourselves treasures upon earth, where moth and rust doth corrupt, and where thieves break through and steal."—Matthew 6:19.

"No man that warreth entangleth himself with the affairs of this life; that he may please him who hath chosen him to be a soldier."—II Timothy 2:4.

Put off unfaithfulness. Put on faithfulness.

"Moreover it is required in stewards, that a man be found faithful."—I Corinthians 4:2.

"O love the LORD, *all ye his saints: for the* LORD *preserveth the faithful, and plentifully rewardeth the proud doer."*—Psalm 31:23.

Put off unforgiveness. Put on a forgiving spirit.

"But if ye do not forgive, neither will your Father which is in heaven forgive your trespasses."—Mark 11:26.

"For if ye forgive men their trespasses, your heavenly Father will also forgive you."—Matthew 6:14.

Put off ungratefulness. Put on thankfulness.

"Because that, when they knew God, they glorified him not as God, neither were thankful, but became vain in their imaginations, and their foolish heart was darkened."—Romans 1:21.

"Giving thanks always for all things unto God and the Father in the name of our Lord Jesus Christ."—Ephesians 5:20.

Put off witchcraft/astrology. Put on listening to the one true God.

"There shall not be found among you any one that maketh his son or his daughter to pass through the fire, or that useth divination, or an observer of times, or an enchanter, or a witch."—Deuteronomy 18:10.

"And I will cut off witchcrafts out of thine hand; and thou shalt have no more soothsayers."—Micah 5:12.

Put off worry and fear. Put on trust in the Lord.

"Therefore I say unto you, Take no thought for your life, what ye shall eat, or what ye shall drink; nor yet for your body, what ye shall put on. Is not the life more than meat, and the body than raiment?"—Matthew 6:25.

"Casting all your care upon him; for he careth for you."—I Peter 5:7.

For a complete list of
available books,
please go to

swordofthelord.com.